San Diego City Schools
Publisher's Review Sample
Return to IMC
School Library Services

616.99   Yount, Lisa.
YOU   Cancer

	DATE DUE	
JE 23 '05		

Cancer

Look for these and other books in the Lucent Overview Series:

Abortion

Alcoholism

Artificial Organs

The Brain

Cancer

Dealing with Death

Depression

Diabetes

Drug Abuse

Drugs and Sports

Eating Disorders

Euthanasia

Genetic Engineering

Memory

Mental Illness

Organ Transplants

Smoking

Cancer

by Lisa Yount

LUCENT
BOOKS

LUCENT *Overview Series*

Library of Congress Cataloging-in-Publication Data

Yount, Lisa.
    Cancer / by Lisa Yount.
        p.   cm. — (Overview series)
    Includes bibliographical references and index.
    Summary: Discusses the effects, causes, prevention, detection,
and treatment of cancer.
    ISBN 1-56006-363-7 (lib. bdg.)
    1. Cancer—Juvenile literature.   I. Title.   II. Series: Lucent
overview series.
    RC264.Y68   1999
    616.99'4—dc21   98-54797
                                                                CIP
                                                                AC

Copyright © 1999 by Lucent Books, Inc.
P.O. Box 289011, San Diego, CA 92198-9011
Printed in the U.S.A.

In memory of my mother,
Agnes Pratt Yount

Contents

INTRODUCTION   8

CHAPTER ONE   11
What Is Cancer?

CHAPTER TWO   21
What Causes Cancer?

CHAPTER THREE   30
What Raises Cancer Risk?

CHAPTER FOUR   43
How Can Cancer Be Prevented?

CHAPTER FIVE   52
How Can Cancer Be Detected?

CHAPTER SIX   60
How Is Cancer Treated?

CHAPTER SEVEN   69
Will Researchers Soon Cure Cancer?

CONCLUSION   79

NOTES   83
GLOSSARY   87
ORGANIZATIONS TO CONTACT   95
SUGGESTIONS FOR FURTHER READING   99
WORKS CONSULTED   101
INDEX   105
PICTURE CREDITS   111
ABOUT THE AUTHOR   111

Introduction

DOCTORS HAVE WRITTEN about cancer since the dawn of recorded history. Descriptions of cancer can be found in the papyrus writings of ancient Egypt and the clay tablets of Babylonia.

Evidence suggests that a famous Greek physician named Hippocrates gave cancer its name about twenty-four hundred years ago. His writings contain the earliest known identification of the disease as *carcinos*, the Greek word meaning "crab." Experts think he chose that word because he saw that a cancerous tumor, or mass of cells, extends "fingers" of tissue into its surroundings. Tumors resemble crabs reaching out their pinching claws. Later, Roman writers translated this Greek word into their own word for "crab," *cancer*.

Although doctors knew about cancer a long time ago, they were seldom able to do much for people who had it. If a tumor was near the surface of the body and fairly small, surgeons could sometimes cut it out. Some doctors tried to burn away tumors with fire or harsh chemicals such as lye. Some gave people medicine with strange ingredients such as toads or violet leaves. A cancer treatment popular for centuries used the deadly poison arsenic. Few of these treatments were successful. Some probably killed the patients before the cancers could.

Most treatments that have real power to cure cancer were developed in the last sixty years. The first effective anticancer drugs and the first techniques for using radiation to treat tumors deep in the body were developed shortly after World War II. In 1971, when President Richard

Nixon declared a "war on cancer," many people thought that cancer would soon be defeated, just as diseases caused by bacteria had seemingly been conquered by antibiotics.

War on cancer not yet won

Despite important advances, the war on cancer has not been won. Indeed, in the 1970s and 1980s, when the war on cancer was being fought vigorously, both the number of cases of cancer diagnosed (identified by doctors) and the number of Americans dying from the disease increased. This resulted in part from new tests that helped doctors detect cancers that would have remained hidden in the past. Also, people were living longer than before, and most cancers strike older people. In addition, many experts feared that environmental factors such as cigarette smoke, pesticides, and industrial chemicals, increased ultraviolet radiation from sunlight because of the reduced ozone layer, and chemical additives in foods were increasing the cancer rate.

Hippocrates is thought to have given the disease cancer *its name.*

The increases in cancer cases and cancer deaths began to reverse in the mid-1990s, but more than 2.3 million Americans a year still learn that they have cancer, and some 560,000 die of it. Cancer is the second greatest cause of death in the United States, and many experts think it will surpass heart and blood vessel disease and become the greatest cause around the year 2000. Science historian Robert Proctor calls cancer "the plague of the 20th century."[1]

Even so, because of what doctors and scientists have learned in recent years, about half the people who get cancer today survive it—and the percentage is growing. Fifty years ago only one-fifth survived. Today more cancers are found early, when they are easier to treat. New drugs and new ways of using radiation, surgery, and even the body's

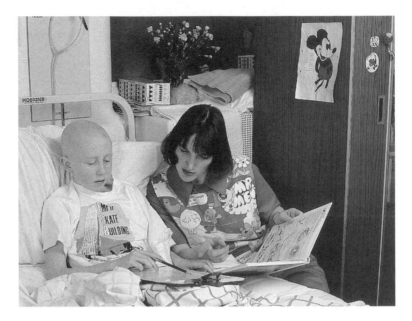

Although cancer is the second greatest cause of death in the United States, improvements in drugs, radiation, and surgery have increased survival rates.

own defense system destroy tumors that could not have been destroyed in the past. New discoveries about factors in the environment and in people's lifestyles that increase or decrease cancer risk can help prevent cancer.

Perhaps most important, scientists for the first time are coming to understand what cancer really is and how it starts. They are learning exactly how body cells and genes change when the cells become cancerous. This information does much more than lay the groundwork for saving more cancer patients' lives, important as that is. "The beautiful thing about research on the causes of cancer," says Philip Leder of Harvard Medical School, "is that it's taught even more about cell biology than it has about cancer."[2] By studying cancer, scientists are learning not only about a deadly disease but about life itself.

1

What Is Cancer?

CANCER CAN STRIKE almost any living thing. Not only mammals but birds, fish, and insects get cancer. Tumors have been found in dinosaur bones, and cancerlike growths appear in plants as well. It could be said that where there is life, there is cancer.

Human beings can get over two hundred kinds of cancer, and each kind is really a different disease. Some progress more rapidly than others and present a greater threat to life. Some are difficult to treat, while others can almost always be cured completely. "We haven't reached where we would like to be in [treating and understanding] cancer . . . because cancer is extraordinarily complex,"[3] says Richard Klausner, the director of the National Cancer Institute, one of the government-sponsored National Institutes of Health in Bethesda, Maryland. Despite their differences, however, all cancers have certain features in common.

Wildly dividing cells

Cells are the microscopic units that make up the bodies of all living things. The human body contains trillions of them. Each cell is surrounded by a thin envelope, or membrane, which separates it from other cells.

Cells grow by dividing, or splitting in two. Some kinds of cells divide often, while others seldom or never divide. Cells in human skin, for example, divide about once a month. Most human brain cells, on the other hand, do not divide after birth. Certain circumstances may speed up division of certain cells, as when skin cells divide to heal a

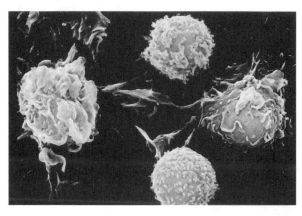

Cancerous tumors send out threads of rapidly dividing cells that invade nearby tissue.

wound, but this change normally lasts for only a short time.

Cells divide only when they receive chemical signals to do so. Other signals make them stop dividing. Most cells also stop dividing when they touch other cells. (This is what tells cells to stop dividing after a wound is closed.) A cancer cell, however, fails to respond to "stop" signals and continues to divide repeatedly. As a result, a single cancer cell soon becomes a clump of cells. This clump, microscopic in size at first, may go on to form a visible tumor.

Sometimes cells divide when they should not, but their number grows slowly. They form *benign* tumors, a word that means "mild" or "gentle." Benign tumors can cause health problems if they grow large and press on nearby organs, but they are not cancerous. Tumors made up of cancer cells are called *malignant* tumors, which means "harmful" or "evil." When the word *tumor* is used in this book, it refers to a malignant tumor, unless the word *benign* is also used.

Ageless cells

Just as young people take on jobs and other responsibilities when they grow up, so do normal cells. Mature cells look and act different from one another because they do different kinds of work in the body. The main job of nerve cells, for example, is to transmit messages. These cells therefore have many long, slender branches that connect with other nerve cells. They contain chemicals that allow them to communicate. Disc-shaped red blood cells do not need these branches or chemicals. Instead, they have a red pigment called hemoglobin, which attaches to oxygen molecules. Hemoglobin lets the red cells do the vital job of carrying oxygen throughout the body.

Cancer cells are the Peter Pans of the cell world (though their behavior is more like that of Peter's enemies, the pirates). In effect, they give up their responsibilities and return to an endless childhood. They lose the power to do particular jobs and lose the appearance and other features that mark mature cells. They become more like the immature cells in unborn babies.

Normal cells also age and eventually die, just as people do. A "program" built into a cell's genes tells the cell to kill itself after it has divided a certain number of times. This program also goes into action if the cell's genes, which contain all of its operating instructions, become damaged. Cancer cells, however, do not respond to the death program. Potentially, they can go on dividing forever. "For an animal to live, it must contain within its cells the knowledge that they have to die," says Samuel Broder, a former director of the National Cancer Institute. "But the cancer cell divides at all cost. It's forgotten how to die."[4]

Invading cells

Normal cells get along like people in a friendly neighborhood. They do not push against one another or take food from one another. Cancer cells, however, break these rules. Just as Hippocrates noticed so long ago, malignant tumors send out threads of rapidly dividing cells to invade nearby tissues. A tissue, such as muscle tissue, is a group of cells that all do the same job.

Unlike most normal cells, cancer cells also can move from one part of the body to another. They break loose from a tumor in one tissue and work their way into blood

Cell division in healthy cells stops when one cell touches another (left). Cancerous cells continue to divide, eventually forming a tumor (right).

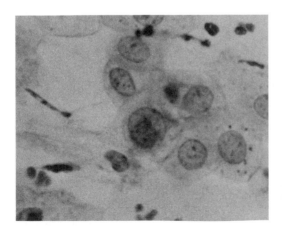
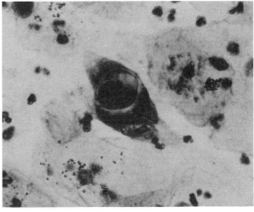

vessels or into the vessels that carry the milky body fluid called lymph. Blood or lymph carries them to other parts of the body. The cells then move out of the vessels and invade a different tissue. Cells from a lung tumor may invade a bone, for example. The cancer cells begin to make a new tumor in this second tissue.

When cancer cells invade a tissue or an organ such as the lung or liver, they push normal cells aside. (Many cancers and some benign tumors cause pain because they push against sensitive nerves.) They damage the cells and keep them from doing their jobs. The cancer cells also develop their own network of blood vessels and take over the blood supply and nutrients intended for the normal cells. In effect, they starve the normal cells to death. Some tumors also produce substances that interfere with the normal working of the body.

This power to form new tumors, or metastases, in different parts of the body is what makes some cancers so deadly and hard to treat. (Benign tumors do not form metastases, and some cancers, such as the more common types of skin cancer, seldom do.) A single tumor often can be removed by surgery or killed by radiation. Once cells from a tumor have spread to other parts of the body, however, finding and destroying all the new groups of cells becomes much more difficult. In time the cancer cells may take over most of the body.

Kinds of cancer

Any kind of cell can become a cancer cell. Cancer therefore can appear in any tissue or organ. Each kind of cancer has its own name, which refers to the kind of cells the cancer came from. For example, the skin cancer called melanoma comes from cells that contain the dark coloring matter called melanin.

Most kinds of cancer form solid tumors. Oncologists, or doctors who study and treat cancer, usually divide such tumors into two large groups. One group is called the carcinomas. (A word ending in -*oma* means a growth or tumor, though not necessarily a cancerous one.) Carcinomas are

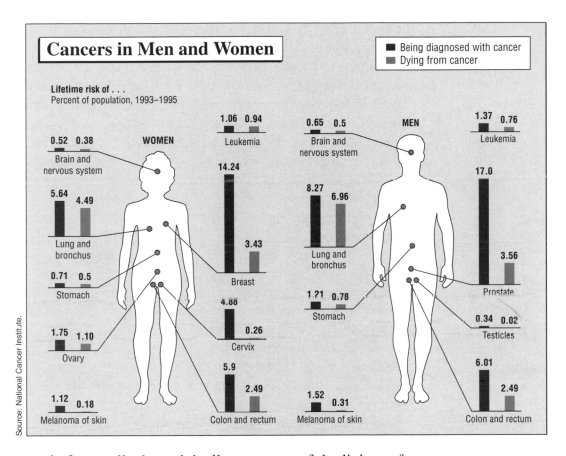

Cancers in Men and Women

■ Being diagnosed with cancer
■ Dying from cancer

Lifetime risk of . . .
Percent of population, 1993–1995

WOMEN

Brain and nervous system
0.52 0.38

Leukemia
1.06 0.94

Lung and bronchus
5.64 4.49

Breast
14.24 3.43

Stomach
0.71 0.5

Cervix
4.88 0.26

Ovary
1.75 1.10

Colon and rectum
5.9 2.49

Melanoma of skin
1.12 0.18

MEN

Brain and nervous system
0.65 0.5

Leukemia
1.37 0.76

Lung and bronchus
8.27 6.96

Prostate
17.0 3.56

Stomach
1.21 0.78

Testicles
0.34 0.02

Melanoma of skin
1.52 0.31

Colon and rectum
6.01 2.49

Source: National Cancer Institute.

made from cells that originally were part of the linings of the body. This includes not only the skin but also the linings inside the body, such as the lining of the digestive system. Most of the common kinds of cancer in the United States are carcinomas. They include lung cancer, breast cancer, and cancer of the colon (part of the large intestine).

Sarcomas make up the second group of solid cancers. *Sarcoma* comes from a Greek word meaning "fleshy tumor." The cells in sarcomas come from the tissues that hold the body together. Tumors of bone or muscle are sarcomas, for example. Sarcomas are rarer than carcinomas.

When cells in blood or other body fluids become cancerous, they usually do not form solid masses. These cancers, too, are named after the cells they came from. Cancers from white blood cells, which make up part of the body's immune, or disease defense, system, are called leukemias.

Cancers from cells in lymph, another part of the immune system, are called lymphomas.

Some kinds of cancer are more common than others, and some are also more likely to be fatal. Cancers of the lung, colon, breast (in women), and prostate (in men) are the most common cancers in North America. Of these, lung cancer is by far the deadliest. In 1996, for example, 177,000 new cases of lung cancer were identified, and 158,700 Americans died of the disease.

The following examples of common cancers show how cancers begin, how they are detected, and how they are treated.

Lung cancer

Lung cancer, a carcinoma, is the most common kind of cancer in American men and the second most common one in women. It most often begins after chemicals in cigarette smoke or polluted air harm cells in the lungs. The first cells to be damaged are those in the lining of the bronchial tubes, which carry air into the lungs. Tiny hairs normally

A cancerous lung. Only 10 percent of lung cancer patients are alive five years after their cancer is diagnosed.

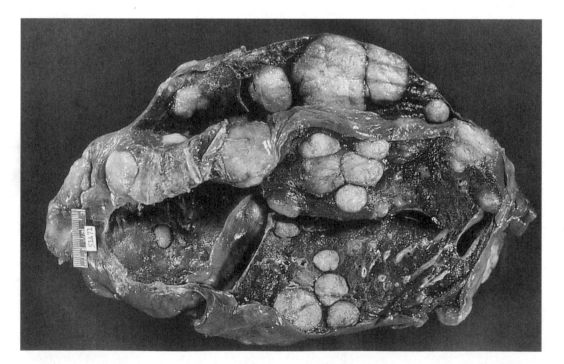

grow from these cells. The hairs whip back and forth constantly, forcing the thick liquid, or mucus, on the lining to keep moving. Chemicals in smoke destroy these hairs. Then the mucus no longer moves and the chemicals stay in one place. Now they can harm other cells in the lungs, and this damage sometimes makes the cells become cancerous.

The first sign of lung cancer is often a cough that lasts a long time and slowly grows worse. The cough happens because the lungs are trying to get rid of the mucus that accumulates. Another common sign is shortness of breath after exercise. Sometimes the person has chest pain or starts to cough up blood. Symptoms, or signs of illness, like these are likely to make the person go to a doctor.

The doctor will send the person to get a chest X ray or perhaps another kind of X-ray image called a CT scan. A lung tumor will show up as a white area on the X-ray picture. If the doctor sees such an area, he or she will look into the person's airways through an instrument called a bronchoscope. The thin, flexible tube of the bronchoscope is put in through the mouth. If the doctor sees a tumor through the bronchoscope, he or she can use special instruments to take a small sample of the tumor. A sample of tissue like this is called a biopsy. Many kinds of cancer are identified by taking and examining biopsies.

The lung biopsy will be sent to a pathologist, or doctor who studies diseased tissue. The pathologist will examine the biopsy under a microscope, looking for cancer cells. The pathologist may also look at mucus the person coughs up to see whether it contains cancer cells.

Unfortunately, lung cancer often causes no symptoms until the tumor has become quite large. By then, cancer cells from the lung often have spread to other parts of the body and started other tumors there. For these reasons, lung cancer is usually very hard to treat. Some lung tumors can be removed by surgery. Radiation or chemotherapy—treatment with anticancer drugs—helps some people whose tumors have spread. Most people who get lung cancer, however, die of it. Only 10 percent of people with lung cancer are alive five years after their cancer has been diagnosed.

Skin cancer

Skin cancer is another common kind of carcinoma. It often begins when skin cells are harmed by ultraviolet rays from sunlight. Some kinds of chemicals also can damage skin cells and start cancer.

Because they are on the surface of the body, skin cancers are usually easy to spot. Their appearance depends on the kind of skin cell that has become malignant. Some show as rough red or brown patches, while others form sores called ulcers (not all ulcers are cancerous, however). The most dangerous kind of skin cancer, malignant melanoma, looks like a mole. (Indeed, a melanoma may start growing in a mole that already exists.) A person who notices an unexplained lump or sore on the skin should see a doctor. So should anyone who sees growth or a change in shape of an existing wart or mole. The doctor will remove the lump, or possibly take a biopsy of it, and send it to a pathologist.

The kinds of skin cancer that appear most often are very easy to treat. A surgeon simply cuts them out or freezes or burns them off. If that is not practical, they may be treated by radiation. These kinds of cancer grow slowly, usually do not spread to other parts of the body, and can be cured completely in almost all cases. (Removing them may leave

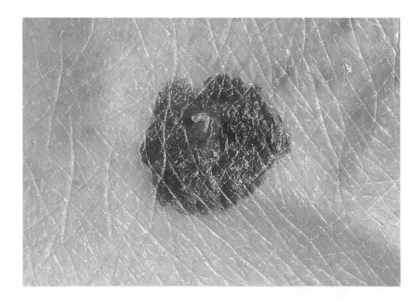

A change of shape in a mole or wart can be a sign of skin cancer.

scars, though.) Melanoma, on the other hand, grows and spreads very rapidly and is hard to treat unless it is caught early. Luckily, it is fairly rare.

Leukemia

Leukemias are cancers of the white cells in the bone marrow (the fatty matter inside the body's major bones, where all blood cells are made) or lymph. These cells normally are part of the immune system. Sometimes, instead of becoming mature, white cells remain immature and go on dividing. High doses of radiation cause some cases of leukemia, and certain chemicals cause others. No one knows what causes most cases.

When leukemia cells start to crowd the bone marrow, they slow the production of other kinds of blood cells. If too few red blood cells are made, body cells do not get enough oxygen. As a result, the person with leukemia feels tired all the time. If too few blood platelets are produced, the blood does not clot well after an injury, so the person may have frequent nosebleeds or bruise easily. Because the leukemic white cells do not do normal white cells' job of defending the body, a person with leukemia may come down with one cold or infection after another.

If a person shows symptoms that suggest leukemia, a doctor will first draw a sample of blood and have it examined for cancer cells. If such cells are found, the bone marrow must be checked. A doctor obtains a biopsy of bone marrow by putting a long, hollow needle into the hip, using a local anesthetic. Biopsies may also be taken of lymph nodes, small pieces of tissue in places such as the armpit and neck that contain large numbers of lymph cells.

Different white blood cells produce different kinds of leukemia. There are four main types, some of which are more common in children (leukemia is the most common kind of childhood cancer), and some in adults. Leukemia is treated with anticancer drugs or, sometimes, transplantation of bone marrow from a donor, usually a close relative. Childhood leukemia, which used to be fatal almost all the time, now can be cured completely in over half of the cases.

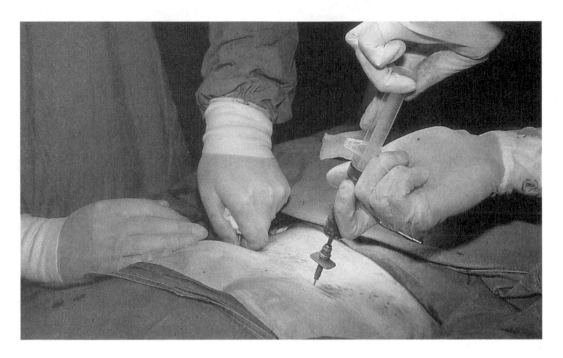

A long, hollow needle inserted in the hip is used to remove bone marrow so it can be tested for cancer cells.

Adult leukemia is harder to cure, but treatments often can produce a remission, or temporary absence of cancer, that lasts for years.

Whatever kind of cancer a person gets, detecting it early offers the best hope of treating it successfully. Regular medical checkups are important for this reason. Avoiding factors that damage cells, such as cigarette smoke and intense sunlight, increase the chances of not getting cancer in the first place.

2

What Causes Cancer?

UNTIL ABOUT TWENTY years ago, cancer was a "black box." No one knew what happened to make a cell become cancerous. Researchers had no idea why some tumors grew slowly and remained in one place while others spread through the body like a forest fire. Today, however, scientists know that all cancers start because of changes in genes.

The cell's computer programs

Genes are the "computer programs" that tell each cell in the body what to do throughout a person's life. A human's 100,000 or so genes are carried in twenty-three pairs of wormlike bodies called chromosomes in the central body, or nucleus, of the cell. Each gene is part of a long, complex molecule of a chemical called deoxyribonucleic acid, or DNA. Each gene usually contains instructions for making one chemical in the cell. The gene's message is encoded in the arrangement of smaller chemicals called bases that make up most of the DNA, just as the meaning of words is encoded in alphabet letters arranged in a certain order.

Genes control all of a cell's activities, including when and how often it divides. Some genes turn others on and off (make them active or inactive). When certain genes are turned on, a cell divides. Turning off those genes and turning on others makes the cell stop dividing.

Living things inherit their genes from their parents. In most living things, including human beings, genes exist in pairs, with one member of each pair coming from the father and one from the mother. The genes are passed along in the sex cells that join to make a new living thing: an egg cell from the mother and a sperm cell from the father.

The genes in each pair often differ slightly from each other because of mutations, or changes in the order of bases, that occurred in the genes of the living thing's ancestors. Mutations can also change genes in individual cells during an organism's lifetime. Chemicals in the cell often repair a new mutation, but not always. When a cell with an unrepaired mutation divides, it passes on the mutation to the two "daughter cells" formed from it. Only mutations that occur in sex cells are passed on to a living thing's descendants, however.

Mutations can modify the structure or amount of the chemical a gene makes, or they can change when the gene turns on or off. Most mutations either kill a cell immediately or have no effect on it. Some mutations, however, allow a cell to survive but change its behavior in profound ways.

Normal cells gone bad

The first hints that genes and mutations had something to do with cancer came in the early 1970s. Scientists had known since early in the century that some viruses could cause cancer in animals. (A few viruses were later found to cause cancer in people, too, but they account for only a small percentage of human cancers.) Around 1970, researchers found two forms of a virus that infected chickens, one of which could cause cancer and one of which could not. The forms differed by only one gene, which the scientists called *src*, for "sarcoma." Since the virus that possessed *src* was the one that made tumors grow in the chickens, the researchers assumed that this gene somehow could cause cancer. They called it an oncogene (*onco-* means "tumor" or "cancer").

At first, everyone thought *src* was a virus gene. In 1975, however, Michael Bishop and Harold Varmus, then work-

ing at the University of California at San Francisco, found that a gene almost exactly like *src* existed in the cells of healthy chickens. They guessed that *src* was a chicken gene that the virus had picked up and added to its own genome, or collection of genes, at some time in the distant past. In the virus, the gene had mutated into a form that caused cancer. Bishop and Varmus won the Nobel Prize in physiology or medicine in 1989 for showing that oncogenes could be mutated forms of normal cell genes.

More and more oncogenes were discovered in the years that followed. (Today, some seventy are known.) Unlike *src*, most did not appear in viruses. The first oncogene proven to play a role in human cancer, called *ras* (for "rat sarcoma," in which it was first identified), was found in human bladder tumors in 1982.

The normal (non-cancer-causing) forms of *src*, *ras*, and other oncogenes proved to be part of the genome of a wide variety of living things, including humans. (As Michael Bishop put it, "We carry the seeds of our cancer within us."[5])

DNA is the molecular basis of heredity. The 100,000 or more genes in the human body are contained in DNA molecules like this.

Michael Bishop, one of two 1989 Nobel Prize winners for discoveries about the behavior of cancer cells.

This fact suggested that these genes did something very important in cells. Beginning in 1983, researchers showed that oncogenes usually stimulate cell growth. In normal cells, other genes or their products turn these genes off when growth is supposed to stop. The cancer-causing forms of oncogenes, however, cause growth to occur continuously.

Missing genes

A kind of eye cancer called retinoblastoma, which blinds young children, showed researchers another way that mutations in genes could cause cancer. In the 1970s, retinoblastoma was one of the few kinds of cancer, all of them rare, that were known to be inherited. However, not all children who developed this form of cancer were related to other people who had the disease.

In 1971, Alfred G. Knudson Jr., then working at the M. D. Anderson Cancer Center in Houston, Texas, guessed that retinoblastoma was caused by mutations in two genes—both members of a pair. Knudson thought that most children with retinoblastoma had inherited a mutated gene from one parent and a normal gene from the other. Then, while their eye cells were multiplying rapidly around the time of birth, a second mutation "knocked out" the normal gene in one eye cell. (Mutations usually occur when a cell is dividing, so the more often a cell divides, the more likely it is to acquire a mutation.) Once both genes in the pair were inactivated by the mutations, that eye cell began to multiply into a tumor. In the few cases when a child with retinoblastoma did not come from a family in which the disease was common, Knudson guessed that two separate mutations had knocked out the crucial genes during the child's early development.

Knudson's "two hit" idea could be no more than an interesting theory until the gene whose existence he had suggested was actually found. Several research laboratories began a hunt for the gene, which they called *Rb*, for "retinoblastoma." In those days, finding a single unknown gene in a human being's large genome was far more difficult than locating the proverbial needle in a haystack, since most of the tools and techniques that scientists now use for this purpose had not yet been invented.

Genes that halt growth

Researchers received an important clue to *Rb*'s location when Jorge Yunis of the University of Minnesota Medical School noticed that part of the thirteenth of the twenty-three human chromosomes was consistently missing in cells from retinoblastoma tumors. This piece was also missing in the normal body cells of children who had inherited the disease, but it was missing only in the tumor cells of children who had not. That fit with Knudson's theory, since an inherited defect would be present in all of an offspring's

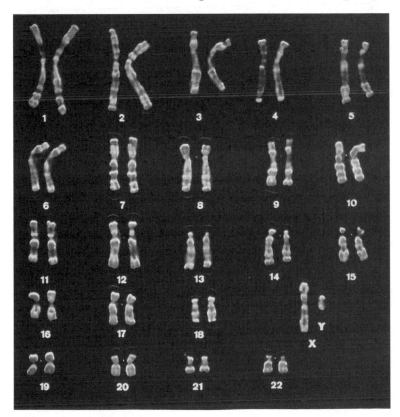

Since new techniques and tools have improved, finding a gene on one of the twenty-three pairs of human chromosomes (pictured) is no longer like looking for a needle in a haystack.

cells but a mutation that occurred later would not. Laboratories began to focus on chromosome 13, and in 1986 Stephen H. Friend and others in the laboratory of Robert Weinberg finally located and cloned the gene (made copies of it for study).

Weinberg and the members of his laboratory at the Whitehead Institute for Biomedical Research in Cambridge, Massachusetts, were already leaders in research on oncogenes. Weinberg realized, however, that *Rb* was, in a way, the opposite of an oncogene. The normal form of an oncogene caused cell division to occur, and the mutated form made it occur constantly. In other words, oncogenes acted like a gas pedal stuck in the down position. The normal form of *Rb*, on the other hand, somehow stopped tumors from appearing, perhaps by stopping cell division. As long as a cell possessed at least one functioning *Rb* gene, it behaved normally. If both *Rb* genes were inactivated by mutations, however, the cell behaved like a car with no brakes. The result was the same: a cancerous tumor.

Rb was the first of a new class of cancer-related genes that came to be called tumor-suppressor genes. *Rb* proved to be missing not only in retinoblastoma but in some cases of much more common cancers, such as those of the breast and lung. Since then, a number of other tumor-suppressor genes have been found. Damaged tumor-suppressor genes seem to be involved in many types of both inherited cancer and cancer that arises because of mutations that occur in cells during a person's lifetime. For instance, a tumor-suppressor gene called p53, discovered by Bert Vogelstein of Johns Hopkins Medical School in 1989, proved to be mutated in over 50 percent of the wide variety of tumors Vogelstein tested. It has since been shown to be involved in fifty-two different kinds of cancer.

Spell checker genes

The first of a third group of cancer-related genes was found in 1993. When a cell divides, it copies its DNA so that both daughter cells will inherit a complete genome. Mistakes can occur during this process, just as someone

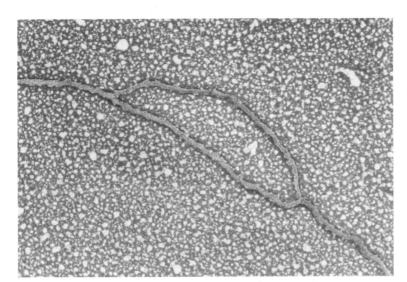

A replicating DNA strand marks the point when mutations can be passed to future generations.

typing text into a computer might make a spelling mistake. Certain genes in normal cells act as spell checkers, detecting and repairing errors. If mutations inactivate one or more of these repair genes, DNA filled with errors is passed on to future generations of cells. If some of the errors are in tumor-related genes, cancer may be the result. "These genes are the mothers of all housekeeping genes,"[6] says Bert Vogelstein, whose laboratory codiscovered the first one in a family with inherited colon cancer.

As scientists have discovered growing numbers of cancer-related genes and have begun to work out the different parts these genes play in normal and cancerous cells, they have come to appreciate just how complex a cell's life cycle is. Turning cell growth on or off requires interactions among dozens of genes and the chemicals they produce, as does a cell's development into a mature form that does a specific job.

A lifetime of damage

A change in any cancer-related gene *can* lead to cancer—but most often it does not. Researchers have learned that mutations in several different genes usually must occur before a cell becomes damaged enough to produce a dangerous tumor. Like a nuclear power plant, a cell has checkpoints and backup systems that usually keep serious problems from arising if a failure (mutation) in one or even several systems occurs. If genes such as p53 or one of the DNA repair genes detect damage or abnormality, they shut down cell division until the damage can be repaired, just as safety systems might shut down part or even all of a nuclear plant's activity if they detect escaping radiation. If the damage is too severe, the cell's protective systems activate the "suicide" program that destroys it. Only if all these backups fail does a cancer, the equivalent of a nuclear accident, appear.

Bert Vogelstein was one of the first to show how complicated the chain of events leading to cancer usually is. In the late 1980s he determined that tumors in the colon go through at least four stages of development, each involving a mutation in a different gene. The process seems to go like this:

1. A growth-suppressor gene on chromosome 5 is destroyed in certain cells in the colon wall; these cells start to multiply faster than normal.

2. The normal form of *ras*, a gene on chromosome 11, mutates into its potentially cancer-causing form. The cells with this mutation form a small tumor called a polyp, which at this stage is benign.

3. Another growth-suppressor gene, this one on chromosome 18, is knocked out. The polyp now grows larger and becomes malignant.

4. A tumor-suppressor gene on chromosome 17 (it proved to be the p53 gene) is damaged. Cells from the malignant polyp now invade the colon wall and begin to spread to other parts of the body.

Recent research has shown that most other cancers result from equally complex processes, each step of which requires a mutation in a different gene. Each mutation gives these cells an evolutionary advantage over their normal neighbors, allowing them to grow faster and capture more space and nutrients, just as criminals who refuse to follow the rules of society may gain at least a temporary advantage over law-abiding citizens. (Like criminals, the cancer cells can lose this advantage either by being stopped through treatment or by harming their "society"—the body—so badly that death results.)

These mutations do not happen all at once. Some people inherit one or more of them, which increases their chance of developing cancer but by no means makes it certain. Other mutations take place during a person's lifetime, caused by chance or by carcinogens (cancer-causing factors in the environment). Different mutations may occur decades apart. Most cancers occur in older people because a lifetime of genetic damage is usually needed to trigger a tumor.

The cancer gene hunt

Researchers continue the work of identifying and trying to understand the genes that can start a cell on the road to cancer. Every year they identify new cancer-related genes; about one hundred such genes, of which at least thirty-six play a part in human tumors, are now known. Researchers are also learning more about the roles that cancer-related genes play in the complex life cycles of normal and cancerous cells. Indeed, in the future, cancers will probably be classified according to the genes that are defective in them rather than the tumors' location.

Whether they painstakingly trace inherited cancers through generations of family trees or apply sophisticated techniques to DNA in a laboratory, nearly all researchers seeking the root cause of cancer today focus on genes. "Most every significant basic research project we fund is seeking to characterize the genes that turn tumor growth on and off," says Richard Klausner of the National Cancer Institute. "That represents a major shift in the direction of cancer research over the past few years."[7]

3

What Raises
Cancer Risk?

Every month or two, it seems, newspaper headlines proclaim that scientists have discovered a new "cause" of cancer—something that damages cells in a way that makes cancerous changes in the cells' genes more likely. Television news shows, too, carry frightening reports about substances in the environment or lifestyle choices that are said to raise the risk of cancer. Sometimes it appears that, as some people complain, everything causes cancer. Are these reports exaggerated scare stories, or is the danger real?

Cancer from the environment

There is no question that the environment affects a person's chances of getting cancer. All cancer starts because of changes in genes, but most researchers believe that only about 5 to 10 percent of cancers result solely from inherited damage. All the rest arise, at least in part, from mutations that occur during people's lifetimes. Some mutations happen randomly, but most are caused by chemicals or other factors in the environment, such as radiation. These factors damage DNA or disrupt cells' activities in other ways that lead to cancer. Anything that can cause such changes is a carcinogen.

Although scientists agree that carcinogens in the environment play a role in causing most cancers, their agreement stops when they try to determine which carcinogens, in which doses, from which sources are responsible for which percentages of different kinds of cancer. For instance, a 1996 report from the Harvard School of Public Health placed most of the cancer blame on lifestyle choices. The report said that 30 percent of cancers are triggered by tobacco use and another 30 percent by poor diet (a diet containing large amounts of fat or inadequate amounts of fruits and vegetables, for instance) and being overweight.

The Harvard researchers believed that only 2 percent of cancers are caused by environmental pollution. Other researchers and advocates, however, feel that the percentage of cancers that result from products of industry and pollution, such as pesticides and smog, is much higher. "We have a cancer epidemic on our hands, and evidence links it to chemicals and pollution in the ecosystem,"[8] says Joe Thornton of the environmental activist group Greenpeace.

Smoking cigarettes greatly increases the risk of lung cancer as well as cancer of the mouth, esophagus, larynx, and other organs.

The deadliest carcinogens

The case against some carcinogens is much clearer than that against others. Cigarette smoke, for example, contains a number of substances that have been shown to cause cancer in laboratory animals. Smoking primarily causes lung cancer, the single worst killer among cancers. Tobacco use also greatly increases the risk of cancers of the mouth, esophagus (the tube that takes food from the throat to the stomach), larynx (voice box), bladder, and several other organs. Even secondhand smoke (smoke from others' cigarettes breathed in by nonsmokers) increases cancer risk. Results of a large study in Europe, announced in October 1998, indicated that long-term exposure to secondhand smoke raised nonsmoking adults' risk of lung cancer by 20 percent.

High-energy radiation is another unquestioned carcinogen. X rays and some other powerful forms of radiation smash into cells like bullets, damaging their DNA in ways that can lead to cancer. The famous early-twentieth-century scientist Marie Curie, a pioneer in the study of radioactive materials, and many survivors of the atomic bombs dropped on Hiroshima and Nagasaki, Japan, in 1945 died from cancer almost surely caused by their exposure to high-energy radiation.

Few people are exposed to the sort of radiation that killed Curie and the bomb survivors, but almost everyone receives doses of a less powerful but still potentially deadly form of radiation: sunlight. Researchers believe that overexposure to the invisible ultraviolet rays in sunlight causes about 90 percent of the cases of the most common kind of skin cancer. It is also a major cause of melanoma, a rarer but more deadly form of the disease. Severe sunburns, especially in childhood, produce the greatest cancer risk, but even the milder cell damage caused by tanning increases the risk to some degree.

Organochlorines: carcinogens or not?

Evidence against some other possible carcinogens is much less strong. A wide variety of chemicals, including food additives, pesticides, and substances in commonly used materials such as plastics, have been accused of being

carcinogens. So have other factors such as the low-intensity electromagnetic fields put out by power lines and electrical appliances. These are usually the factors that make the scary headlines, yet some researchers deny their dangers as vigorously as others proclaim them.

A typical recent debate has centered on chemicals called organochlorines, complex substances that include the elements carbon and chlorine. Organochlorines are part of many pesticides, certain kinds of incinerator waste, and some plastics. Some organochlorines, such as the pesticide DDT, have been shown to cause cancer or other severe health problems in animals and have been banned in the United States. These chemicals persist in the environment, however, and traces of them appear in the bodies of most living things. Other organochlorines are still widely used in industry.

Organochlorines and certain other chemicals disrupt the action of hormones, the body's long-distance chemical messengers. Hormones control reproduction, the development of young, and many other vital functions. Hormone-disrupting chemicals have been shown to cause abnormal

Pesticides such as DDT have been shown to cause cancer and other health problems in animals.

sexual organs, reproductive failure, and severe birth defects in wildlife. Some scientists strongly suspect them of causing similar problems in humans.

Hormone disruption by organochlorines may also increase the risk of certain kinds of human cancer, especially breast cancer. A widely publicized 1994 study by the New York State Department of Health found that almost 15 percent of Long Island women with breast cancer had lived within one kilometer (.6 miles) of a rubber, chemical, or plastics plant. These types of industry often produce organochlorine-containing waste that can enter air or water. The health department concluded that living near such plants raised a woman's breast cancer risk by 62 percent. "If this association proves real, it will be the first time that an environmental risk factor [for breast cancer] that is avoidable has been identified,"[9] said state health commissioner Mark Chassin. Other studies suggest a link between organochlorine pollution and a recent rise in cancer of the testicles in men.

The relationship between organochlorines and cancer is far from clear, however. These substances can definitely affect human hormone systems, but none of them, especially in the small doses to which people would normally be exposed, has been proven to cause human cancer. Even Theo Colborn, a World Wildlife Fund scientist who believes strongly in the dangers of hormone-disrupting chemicals, said in a 1998 interview that she thought the link between these compounds and breast cancer was "very weak, very poor."[10] As with many other suspected carcinogens, uncertainty still exists about whether, or how much, organochlorines increase human cancer risk.

Are power lines dangerous?

A type of radiation given off by electric power lines and appliances has also been suspected of raising the risk of cancer. Whenever electricity flows through these devices, they radiate electromagnetic energy out in all directions. The radiation within these invisible spheres of energy, called fields, is much weaker and of a different type than the high-energy radiation known to cause cancer. Nonetheless, some people fear that electromagnetic fields (EMFs) can also pose a cancer threat under some conditions.

Concern about EMFs began in 1979, when Nancy Wertheimer and Ed Leeper published a report of research they had done in Denver, Colorado. They visited the homes of children who had died of cancer between 1950 and 1973 to try to determine why these children and not others had become sick. They noticed that an unusually high number of the children lived near electric power lines. Overall, they found, children who lived near high-power lines were twice as likely to have developed cancer (usually leukemia) as those who did not.

Later concern extended to the much weaker EMFs that surround electrical appliances, from electric blankets to computers and TV sets. The more current an appliance uses, the larger its field is and the more energy the field

Though unproven, the possibility that electromagnetic fields created by power lines increase cancer risks remains a concern.

contains. The closer a person is to the appliance, the more exposure to the field he or she receives. A person sleeping two feet away from an electric clock, for example, receives four times as much radiation from the clock's EMF as someone sleeping four feet away, though the amount is still very small.

Debate on EMFs continues

Most current evidence suggests that EMFs around power lines and electrical appliances present little, if any, threat to human health. In 1995 the American Physical Society, the world's largest group of physicists, announced that it could find no evidence that EMFs around power lines increased cancer risk. The National Research Council, part of the prestigious National Academy of Sciences, made a similar statement in 1996, basing its claim on examination of over five hundred different studies. A third large study came to the same conclusion in 1997.

Concern over EMFs refuses to die, however. Another government task force, the National Institute of Environmental Health Sciences, claimed in late 1998 that, in its opinion, EMFs should be considered a possible human carcinogen, at least in children. Furthermore, laboratory studies have suggested some ways that EMFs could affect cells to increase cancer risk. One such study says that EMFs, like organochlorines, can disrupt hormones. Another shows that they can activate some of the same cell chemicals that certain oncogenes do. It is clear that questions about increased cancer risk from EMFs have not yet been answered to everyone's satisfaction.

Testing possible carcinogens

It is no surprise that scientists disagree about the cancer risk from substances in the environment. Giving people suspected carcinogens and waiting to see whether they develop cancer would be unethical because it would deliberately endanger their health, so researchers must get information about carcinogens' effects on humans indirectly. None of the methods they use is completely reliable.

If a factor is suspected of being a carcinogen, scientists can test it in a laboratory. They may apply it to cultures—groups of human or animal cells in test tubes or dishes. They let the cultures grow for a while, then examine the cells under a microscope for signs of cancer. They may also identify chemical or genetic changes in the cells.

Researchers also test suspected carcinogens on laboratory animals such as rats or mice. In such tests, one group of animals is exposed to the suspected factor. If the factor is a chemical, it might be put in the animals' food or painted on their skin. Another group of animals is not exposed to the factor. The two groups are chosen to be as genetically similar as possible, and they are treated in exactly the same way except for exposure to this one factor.

After a certain length of time, the two groups of animals are examined for tumors. If, in test after test, the animals exposed to the factor get far more tumors than those not exposed to it, the factor is considered a carcinogen. The evidence is especially strong if a factor produces tumors in several different species of animals.

Can laboratory tests be trusted?

The Food and Drug Administration (FDA) and the Environmental Protection Agency (EPA), the federal government agencies that protect Americans' food, medicines, and environment, depend primarily on laboratory tests to determine whether a chemical or other substance is a carcinogen. Because the tests are performed on small animals, mathematical calculations are used to "scale up" the results to apply to humans.

Some researchers do not entirely trust laboratory tests, however. They point out that the kinds of cells that grow dependably in the laboratory have already undergone changes that make them more likely than normal cells to become cancerous. Such cells might respond more strongly or quickly to carcinogens than normal cells would.

Similarly, although all mammals (the group of living things to which both humans and most laboratory animals belong) are alike in basic ways, there are important

Although useful, animal testing cannot duplicate real-world conditions in humans.

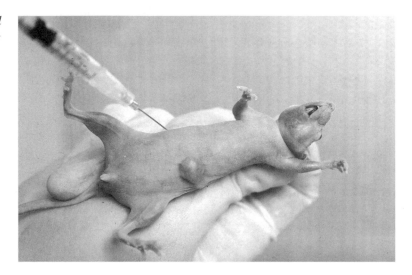

differences between mice and people. "We must reject the . . . simplification that 'a mouse is a little man,'"[11] says Elizabeth Whelan, president of the American Council on Science and Health. Mice can survive doses of some drugs twenty times as high (in proportion to body weight) as humans can, for example. Yet mice may be more sensitive than humans to certain other compounds.

Another problem is that researchers usually give laboratory animals much higher doses of suspected carcinogens, in proportion, than humans are ever likely to consume. Cancer scientist F. Jay Murray explains,

> What regulatory agencies are concerned about is very low risk, the theoretical one in a million. But if we try to figure what dose causes one cancer in a million individuals, you'd need more than a million rats in a test, and no one can do that. So we test on 50 or 100 rats, use much higher doses, then assume we can draw a straight line down [to] what happens at low doses. But it's just not that simple.[12]

Some critics of animal tests point out that high doses of almost any substance can cause health damage that would not occur with low doses. "The dose makes the poison," they say. Berkeley researcher Bruce Ames insists that "The high dose itself causes cancer [by killing cells and encouraging other cells to divide as a healing measure], and most chemicals pose no risk—zero risk—at low doses."[13]

Other critics say that animal tests are not sensitive enough. The tests study only one carcinogen at a time, usually given in a single exposure. Most humans, by contrast, are exposed over long periods to hundreds of known or suspected carcinogens. "We live in a soup," admits Linda Birnbaum, a high-ranking EPA official. "Nobody's exposed to a single chemical or at a single instant in time. It's continuous and it's multiple chemicals."[14] Some of these substances might be harmless in a single low dose but still increase cancer risk significantly if a person receives many exposures or if several carcinogens boost one another's actions. The present form of animal tests cannot detect these kinds of effects.

Disease detectives

While some researchers test carcinogens in the laboratory, others try to identify environmental causes of human cancer in a different way. These scientists, called epidemiologists, are the detectives of the medical world. Some

compare the lives of people who develop cancer with the lives of those who do not, trying to find out whether the people with cancer were exposed to something that the people without cancer were not exposed to. For example, many of the people with a certain kind of cancer may have worked at a particular job. People with another kind of cancer may have eaten large amounts of a food that other people did not eat. Nancy Wertheimer, whose report started concern about the danger of EMFs, was an epidemiologist who studied cancer in this way.

Other epidemiologists keep track of people who have been accidentally exposed to a suspected carcinogen. They find out how many of these people develop tumors in later years and compare that number with the number of people leading similar lives who develop tumors but were not exposed to the carcinogen. From such data they calculate the increased risk of cancer produced by that dose of carcinogen.

Epidemiology, too, has its critics. Two sets of laboratory animals can be treated in exactly the same way except for exposure to one factor, but people cannot. Workers in the

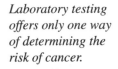

Laboratory testing offers only one way of determining the risk of cancer.

same factory, for instance, differ in eating, drinking, smoking, and other habits. Because people are exposed to so many different environmental factors each day, it is very hard to say which factor or factors caused a certain group of cancers. For instance, the children in Wertheimer and Leeper's study might have developed cancer because of some factor that they had in common other than exposure to EMFs, such as exposure to heavy air pollution.

Those who defend laboratory testing and epidemiology as ways of identifying carcinogens insist that both approaches, although not perfect, are reliable if applied carefully. They also point out that complete proof that a certain agent is harmless may be impossible. As Charles Stevens, head of the National Research Council study that found no evidence for a link between EMFs and cancer, told an interviewer, "No test or study can prove that any environmental agent is safe. All that science can do is . . . show that there is no current evidence of harm."[15]

Still, researchers are trying to improve the accuracy of carcinogen testing. They are also looking for ways to include more compounds in the tests and to measure effects on especially sensitive members of the population, such as children and fetuses (unborn babies). "We have to begin to think smarter,"[16] says Linda Birnbaum.

What should be done about carcinogens?

Many people do not want to wait for absolute proof that certain factors in the environment cause human cancer. "If we wait for the proof, we're all dead,"[17] says Frank Wiewel, president of a grassroots group called People Against Cancer. Such people urge the FDA and the EPA to tighten regulations to keep known or suspected carcinogens from contaminating food, water, air, and workplaces. "There is enough evidence to take certain chemicals off the market today," Theo Colborn maintains, "and we should. But we are not moving on that."[18]

On the other hand, critics such as Elizabeth Whelan point out that attempting to remove all substances that could possibly pose a cancer risk may be impractical at best and harmful at worst. If most pesticides were banned, for example, the amount of plant food available to humans would probably drop because pest insects would consume a larger percentage of farmers' crops than they do now. The price of the remaining food would rise. Poor families then might not be able to afford fruits and vegetables, which may help to prevent cancer. Similarly, if energy companies had to spend a lot of money moving or shielding power lines, they would pass these costs on to consumers in the form of higher prices for electricity. Electric power might then become too expensive for some families.

Disagreement about the amount of cancer risk that various environmental factors present is sure to continue. So is disagreement about what to do about carcinogens once they are identified. Both scientists and American consumers will have to do some hard thinking about these issues in years to come.

4

How Can Cancer Be Prevented?

MANY PEOPLE THINK that nothing can be done to avoid cancer. Among experts, however, science historian Robert N. Proctor writes, "Nearly everyone agrees cancer is a preventable disease."[19] Many researchers believe that at least half the cancer deaths and about two-thirds of the cancer cases in the United States could be prevented. No one can guarantee that he or she will never get cancer, but people can take steps to greatly reduce their cancer risk.

Lifestyle choices

Most methods of reducing cancer risk involve making lifestyle choices that avoid exposure to carcinogens. Chief among these choices is not using tobacco. Those who have started smoking should do their best to quit. People should avoid secondhand smoke whenever possible as well. Tobacco in other forms, such as chewed (smokeless) tobacco, is also dangerous. If everyone gave up tobacco use, scientists estimate that about 30 percent of cancer deaths in the United States could be prevented.

Protecting oneself from the sun is another way of reducing cancer risk. Wearing sunscreen helps, but many researchers feel that this is not enough. They recommend wearing long-sleeved clothing and hats and, if possible, avoiding the sun entirely between the hours of 10 A.M. and 2 P.M., when its ultraviolet rays are most powerful. Marie-Josee Thibault, a surgeon who treats skin conditions at the

University of California at Los Angeles, says, "There's no such thing as a healthy [skin] tan."[20]

A healthy diet

Many other cancer-prevention tips involve diet. Researchers disagree about what role particular foods or types of food play in either causing or preventing cancer, but most advisers recommend avoiding a diet high in fat, especially animal fat. Fat, they say, should make up no more than 30 percent of one's diet, and 20 percent is better. People should also avoid high-calorie diets that lead to obesity (a person who is more than 20 percent over his

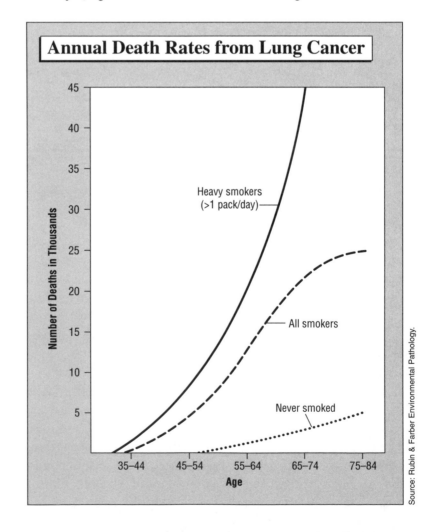

Annual Death Rates from Lung Cancer

or her ideal body weight is considered obese). Obesity has been linked with increased risk of colon cancer and possibly cancers of the uterus (womb), ovaries, and breast in women.

Drinking alcohol moderately or not at all can also lower cancer risk. People who have more than two alcoholic drinks a day have an increased risk of cancers of the mouth, throat, esophagus, and breast. Cutting down on charred, smoked, salted, and pickled foods is also a good idea, because these foods contain carcinogens that contribute to stomach and perhaps other types of cancer.

At least five servings a day of fruits and vegetables may help prevent cancer.

What people do—or at least should—eat is at least as important as what foods they avoid to prevent cancer. Most researchers agree that the most important part of a cancer-prevention diet is a large amount of fruits and vegetables. They recommend eating at least five servings a day, with a serving being defined as half a cup of cooked vegetables or juice, or one average-sized fruit. Fruits and vegetables contain a variety of substances that seem to prevent cancer in animal tests. Broccoli, cauliflower, and related vegetables, for example, contain chemicals called bioflavonoids, which are thought to reduce the risk of colon cancer. Vegetables and other unrefined plant foods, such as beans and brown rice, also contain fiber, or indigestible plant material. Diets high in fiber seem to lower the risk of colon cancer. Experts recommend twenty-five to thirty grams of fiber a day.

Genetic testing

Because of the increased knowledge about the roles some genes play in cancer, scientists have begun to use genetic testing as a form of cancer prevention. Tests that identify mutated genes associated with a greatly increased risk of breast, colon, thyroid, skin, and a few other cancers are now commercially available. For instance, one test identifies people who have inherited mutated forms of genes

AGE-SPECIFIC PROBABILITIES OF DEVELOPING BREAST CANCER		
If current age is:	Then the probability of developing cancer in the next 10 years is:	or 1 in:
20 years	0.04%	2,500
30 years	0.40%	250
40 years	1.49%	67
50 years	2.54%	39
60 years	3.43%	29

Source: American Cancer Society, Surveillance Research, 1997 Data from SEER.

called BRCA1 and BRCA2. If a woman inherits a damaged form of one of these tumor-suppressor genes, she has up to an 85 percent risk of developing breast cancer by age seventy (as compared with an average woman's 10 percent risk) and up to a 50 percent risk of developing ovarian cancer (as compared with an average woman's 1 percent risk). Men who inherit a damaged BRCA gene probably have an increased risk of cancer of the prostate, a male reproductive organ.

Genetic tests can prevent cancer, or at least cancer deaths, by alerting bearers of these mutated genes to their extra risk. These people can then have themselves tested for cancer more often or at a younger age than most people need to be. This increases the chance of spotting the disease early, when it can be most easily treated. These people can also make lifestyle choices that partly offset the risk conferred by their genes. If a person's cancer risk is extremely high, doctors may even recommend that he or she have certain organs removed before they become diseased. By contrast, members of high-risk families who learn that they do not carry a mutated gene can be saved a lifetime of worry and perhaps depression or unnecessary surgery.

The dangers of knowing too much

Even though genetic tests can be useful, most cancer experts presently recommend them only for people with many relations who have or have had cancer. The experts say that if such people are tested, they should be given genetic counseling to help them interpret and deal with the results of the test. If genetic testing is not used carefully, researchers warn, the tests may do more harm than good.

Many people in high-risk families join doctors in having doubts about the wisdom of genetic testing and have decided that they do not want to be tested for cancer genes. In a study of families with a strong history of breast and ovarian cancer who were already taking part in genetic research, for example, less than half (43 percent) of the eligible family members chose to be tested for mutated BRCA1.

There are several reasons for using genetic tests with caution. First, doctors often can do little to lower people's cancer risk once it is identified, and the steps that are possible are drastic, such as removal of healthy organs. Unless

Women who have a high incidence of breast cancer in their families are encouraged to take preventive measures because of their high risk of developing the disease.

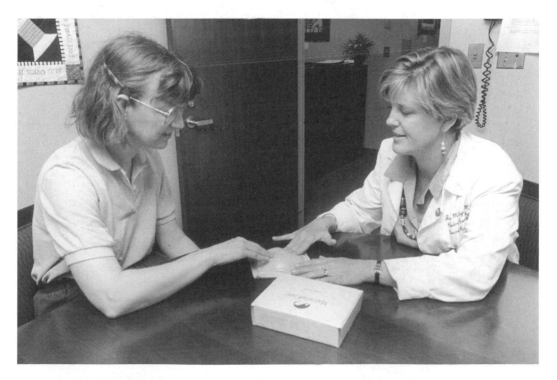

careful counseling is given, learning that one has a cancer-related mutation can lead to depression and even thoughts of suicide. Learning that one has not inherited a dangerous gene, on the other hand, can lead to feelings of guilt or a false sense of safety. A person who does not have the mutation being tested for might have inherited a different but equally dangerous mutation or might develop cancer as a result of mutations that occur during the person's lifetime. Finally, genetic testing can be frustrating because the results often cannot show for sure whether a person has a cancer-causing mutation.

Another danger is that people identified as having a cancer-related mutation may have trouble getting health insurance or be forced to pay a higher price for it. Because many employers provide health insurance for their employees, this problem could extend to difficulty in getting jobs. Discrimination against people with genes that make them more likely than average to develop cancer or other serious diseases "could be the new civil rights issue in

KIRK ©92

I'M SORRY, MR. FEATHERTON... YOU'RE JUST TOO DARN SICK TO GET HEALTH INSURANCE.

this country,"[21] Republican congressman Cliff Stearns of Florida said in 1996.

Even though most people do not need to have genetic testing, cancer experts recommend that people try to learn the causes of the illnesses and deaths of their relatives. Finding that one or two relatives had cancer does not mean much, especially if the people developed the disease in old age, but learning that three or four close relatives had the disease fairly early in life may be a tip-off that a defective cancer-related gene "runs in the family." Knowing one's family history can help to prevent cancer deaths by suggesting when genetic tests or more frequent screening tests for certain types of cancer may be needed.

A cancer-preventing drug

Some researchers are looking for methods other than surgery to prevent cancer in people with inherited mutations that make them likely to develop the disease. One such method seems to have been found. A drug called tamoxifen blocks activity of the female hormone estrogen in breast tissue and, according to several studies, greatly reduces the risk of developing breast cancer in women at high risk because of family history. One study showed that taking tamoxifen reduced incidence of the cancer by 45 percent, compared with the incidence in women at equally high risk who took an inactive placebo, or "dummy pill."

Tamoxifen has been used for years to treat breast cancer and to reduce the chances of a second tumor developing in women who have had one breast removed because of the disease. In October 1998 the FDA also approved its use to prevent breast cancer in women who have never had the disease but are at very high risk of developing it. "For the first time in history," says Bernard Fisher of Allegheny University of the Health Sciences in Pittsburgh, "breast cancer can be not only treated but also prevented."[22] Animal studies suggest that tamoxifen may also prevent prostate cancer in men.

Tamoxifen is not perfect, however. It increases the activity of estrogen in the uterus and more than doubles the risk

Some doctors urge women who have a family history of breast cancer to try preventive drugs.

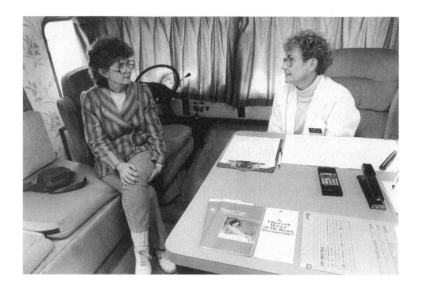

of cancer in that organ. It also almost doubles the risk of potentially fatal blood clots in the lung. Because of these problems, doctors are likely to recommend it for cancer prevention only to women whose genetics or family history places them at a very high risk of breast cancer. A newer synthetic hormone drug, raloxifene, may provide tamoxifen's benefits without increasing the risk of uterine cancer.

Tamoxifen and raloxifene are among several drugs given in the hope of preventing new tumors in people who have had certain kinds of cancer. These drugs seem to encourage precancerous cells to return to normal, stop multiplying, or kill themselves. Some, like tamoxifen, may eventually also be given to healthy people who have a high risk of developing certain kinds of cancers or show precancerous changes in certain tissues or organs.

New stress on prevention

Proof of lowered cancer risk is greater for some cancer-prevention methods than for others. Some methods are also safer or easier to follow than others. Genetic testing and drugs like tamoxifen, for instance, are clearly not for everyone. On the other hand, most of the lifestyle choices recommended for preventing cancer are fairly easy to carry out and are likely to improve health in other ways, so it is wise for most people to follow them. Not smoking and eating a low-fat diet reduce the risk of heart and circulatory diseases as well as cancer, for example. R. Grant Steen of St. Jude's Children's Research Hospital in Memphis, Tennessee, writes, "Much of what we know about cancer prevention is common sense."[23]

Some anticancer groups also urge people to ask their legislators to make reduction of environmental carcinogens more of a major part of cancer prevention. They point out that removing toxic substances from food, air, water, and workplaces can help prevent other diseases as well as cancer.

Critics have pointed out that research on ways to prevent cancer has lagged behind attempts to find causes and cures. This may have occurred partly because, unlike treatments that give promise of curing cancer, new methods of prevention do not make headlines or produce dramatic personal accounts. "A cancer cured [is] a tangible success," Robert Proctor writes; "a cancer prevented [is] invisible, a statistical abstraction. Who would testify on talk shows or before Congress that they [are] alive and well as a result of a well-planned program of preventive medicine?"[24] In the long run, however, many scientists believe that better prevention methods will save far more lives than cures—and without the pain, destruction, and loss of time and money usually involved in treating cancer after it develops.

5

How Can Cancer Be Detected?

THE FIRST STEP toward curing cancer is detecting it. The earlier a cancer is found, the better the chances are that it can be controlled or cured completely. A cancer that is found early has not had time to damage nearby tissues or spread to distant ones. Finding tumors early is easier or more important in some kinds of cancer than others, but early detection is helpful in treating all kinds of cancer.

Warning signs and checkups

The cheapest and easiest way to detect possible cancer is to notice changes that occur in one's own body. The American Cancer Society lists seven cancer warning signs that people should watch for:
- Change in bowel or bladder habits
- A sore that does not heal
- Unusual bleeding or discharge (flow of liquid)
- Thickening or lump in the breast or elsewhere
- Indigestion or difficulty in swallowing
- Obvious change in a wart or mole
- Nagging cough or hoarseness

None of these symptoms means that a person has cancer. Many people have some of them for a short time for other reasons, such as a cold or the flu. They do mean what the first letters of the warning list spell out: CAUTION. A person who has any of these symptoms for more than a few days should see his or her doctor.

Even if a person has none of these warning signs, regular visits to a doctor play a vital part in spotting cancer early. The doctor's examination can sometimes pick up danger signs that patients miss. Most doctors recommend yearly visits for young people, whose bodies are changing rapidly, and for people over age fifty, who are more likely to develop cancer than younger people. A visit once every two years is usually enough for healthy young and middle-aged adults.

Doctors or other health professionals use two types of tests to look for cancer: screening tests and detection tests. Screening tests are done on people who seem to be healthy and have no signs of cancer. These tests are designed to find cancers too small to cause any symptoms. Detection tests are done on people who have symptoms that might be caused by cancer. Their purpose is to find out whether the symptoms are caused by cancer or by something else. If a tumor is present, these tests also help to find it.

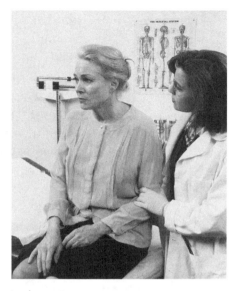

Regular doctor visits can help detect cancer in its early stages.

Screening tests

Screening tests have the advantage of spotting some kinds of cancer in very early stages. Their disadvantage is that most of the people on whom they are used will not need them. In other words, those people will not have cancer.

The ideal screening test must, above all, be reliable. It must find nearly all cancers of the type it is designed to detect, and it must not give abnormal readings when cancer is not present. It should also detect a kind of cancer that is common and easily curable in early stages. Finally, the test should be inexpensive, painless (or nearly so), and easy to use. Most doctors agree about these standards, but they sometimes disagree about which existing tests, if any, truly meet them.

One of the most common cancer screening tests is the Pap test, which detects cancer of the cervix, or neck of the uterus, in women. It is named after its inventor, a Greek physician named Papanicolau. In this test, a doctor obtains a sample of vaginal fluid from a woman during an office visit. Laboratory technicians study the fluid under a microscope, looking for abnormal cells. If such cells are found, other tests can be used to find out whether cancer is present.

The Pap test fulfills most of the standards for a good screening test, and most doctors recommend that all adult women have the test every year or two. However, some are concerned about the number of mistaken or unclear results that the test can give. New methods are being introduced that may make Pap tests more accurate.

Another common screening test, usually given to people over fifty, checks for blood in bowel movements. Such blood can be a sign of colon cancer. People collect small samples for the test at home, and the samples are sent to a laboratory. The test is painless, inexpensive, and usually reliable, and it detects a kind of cancer that is fairly common in older people and often can be treated early. Thus, it too, is a good screening test.

Mammograms and PSA tests

There is more disagreement about the usefulness of some other screening tests. For instance, doctors disagree about mammography, a screening test for breast cancer. This test uses low doses of X rays, which make an image called a mammogram. Lumps in the breast that might be cancerous show up in the picture. Mammography can detect lumps the size of a pinhead, which is much smaller than any that a woman or her doctor could feel. About 90 percent of breast cancers can be cured if they are found when they are this small or only a little larger. Mammography meets most of the requirements for a good screening test, except perhaps for expense. Disagreement arises not about the test itself but about which women should have it.

Most doctors agree that most women under forty years of age do not need mammograms, unless they have close relatives with breast cancer. Doctors also agree that women over fifty should have a mammogram once a year, because most breast cancer occurs in older women. Some studies have shown that yearly mammograms can cut the death rate from breast cancer by about 30 percent in women over fifty.

Questions arise about mammography for women between ages forty and fifty, however. The American Cancer Society and the American Medical Association recommend that women in this age group have a mammogram every one to two years, but the National Cancer Institute dropped a similar recommendation in 1993. In 1997 a panel of experts assembled by the National Institutes of Health concluded that there was not enough evidence to decide the issue. Each woman in this age group, it said, would have to make up her own mind about whether she needed the test.

The prostate-specific antigen (PSA) test, a blood test often given to screen men over fifty for prostate cancer, has also caused debate. Fernand Labrie, a Canadian researcher, estimates that this test, which looks for a substance in the blood that increases when prostate cancer is present, could prevent twenty-seven thousand of the thirty-nine thousand deaths from this cancer each year in the United States if all men over fifty received the test yearly. Other experts, however, say that positive results on the test may cause some men to have surgery or other treatments that they do not really need. These critics point out that some forms of

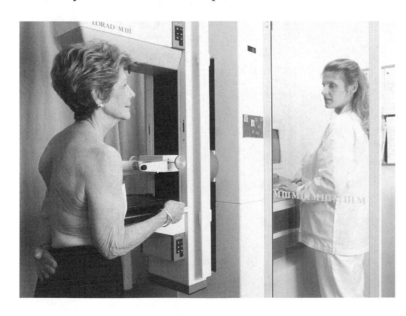

A mammogram can detect a lump the size of a pinhead, which is smaller than a woman or a doctor can feel.

prostate cancer grow so slowly that people who have it usually die of other causes before the cancer becomes large enough to be a serious threat.

Detection tests

Detection tests are performed on people who have symptoms that suggest cancer or on people who have had cancer before. In these latter people the tests can show whether the cancer has returned after treatment. Detection tests are often more difficult or expensive than screening tests. Unlike screening tests, however, they are performed only when there is some medical reason to believe they are needed.

One cancer detection test entails swallowing or injecting a special dye to make soft tissues show up on X rays.

Several kinds of detection tests use X rays. People must swallow or be injected with special dyes before taking some of these tests. The dyes make soft tissues such as blood vessels and digestive organs show up in X-ray pictures.

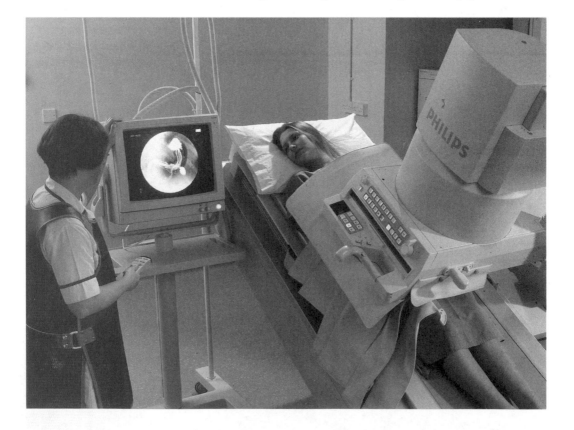

One X-ray test that does not use dyes is the computerized axial tomography (CAT) or CT scan. A CT image is composed of many pictures taken from different angles and combined by a computer. It shows a cross section, or "slice," through the body. Like other X-ray detection tests, CT scans allow doctors to see deep inside a person's body without surgery.

Magnetic resonance imaging (MRI) is another imaging technique used to detect some kinds of deep tumors. The person being tested lies on a table that slides inside a large machine. The MRI machine surrounds the person with a powerful magnetic field, which causes temporary, harmless changes in the atoms of the body. The atoms in cancer cells react differently to the field than the atoms in normal cells do. The machine detects the reactions of the atoms and feeds information about them into a computer. The computer turns the data into a three-dimensional image of part of the body.

Another type of detection test is a CAT or CT scan. This procedure allows the doctor to see deep inside a person's body without surgery.

The advantage of MRI is that it does not use X rays, which present some health risk, especially to pregnant women. It also is better than CT scans at finding tumors in some parts of the body. However, only large hospitals or medical centers are likely to have MRI machines, whereas many hospitals now have CT scanners. The MRI test is also even more expensive than a CT scan.

Supersensitive tests

Even the best screening and detection tests usually can find only tumors that have been growing for some time. Researchers are working to develop much more sensitive tests that may be able to spot tumors while they are still nearly microscopic in size. One blood test, which uses substances called antibodies to detect cells released into the blood by tumors, is said to be able to detect a single cancer cell among 100,000 to 1 million blood cells. The more of these cells that are found in the blood, the more widespread the cancer is likely to be.

Other experimental tests look for some of the changed genes involved in cancer. Rather than detecting inherited genes that increase the risk of cancer, these tests spot changes that occur only after cells have started down the path toward tumor formation. One such test looks for the mutated *ras* oncogene in colon or lung cells. Another looks for p53 mutations in skin, bladder, or other tissues. These tests, if perfected and put into widespread use, may be helpful not only in detecting cancer but in helping doctors determine how dangerous a particular cancer is. Cancers with damaged p53 genes, for instance, are very hard for standard anticancer drugs to kill and may require extra treatment.

The biopsy

If screening or detection tests suggest that someone has cancer, the person's doctor will take a biopsy, or tissue sample, from the suspected tumor. If the tumor is near the surface of the body, the biopsy often can be performed in the doctor's office. If the tumor is deeper, surgery in a hospital may be required.

If a suspected tumor is in a hollow organ, the biopsy may be obtained by using a long, flexible tube called an endoscope. An endoscope is most often inserted through the mouth or rectum. Endoscopes can look into organs such as the bladder, colon, esophagus, and lungs.

An endoscope contains fibers that transmit light. A doctor looks through the endoscope to find the tumor. Many endoscopes also include instruments like scissors that can be used by remote control. If a doctor sees a tumor through the endoscope, he or she presses a trigger and the scissors snip a bit of tissue from it.

After a biopsy is taken, it is sent to a laboratory. Technicians study it with a microscope, looking for cancer cells. Looking at cells from a tumor or other suspect tissue is the only sure way to tell whether the tissue is cancerous.

6

How Is
Cancer Treated?

DOCTORS HAVE COME a long way since the days
when cancer treatments consisted of arsenic paste or
ground-up toads. Most of that progress has taken place
during the last sixty years. Because of progress in treatment
as well as early detection, the overall cure rate for cancer
has gone from 38 percent in the 1960s to 50 percent today.
People are usually considered to be cured of cancer if they
survive for five years without a return of the disease.

The three main ways of treating cancer are surgery, radiation, and chemotherapy (treatment with drugs). The type
of treatment a doctor chooses will depend on the kind of
cancer a person has and how advanced the disease is—
whether it has spread to more than one part of the body, for
instance. The effects of the treatment will depend largely
on these same factors.

Even when cancer is not cured, treatment can extend
and improve patients' lives. It might give months or years
of remission—time during which no cancer can be detected. If remission is not possible, treatment may still
shrink tumors and make patients feel better.

Reducing side effects

Unfortunately, all three types of anticancer treatment destroy healthy cells as well as cancerous ones. Surgeons
usually remove normal tissue around a tumor to increase
the chances of capturing cancer cells that have started to

spread. Radiation and anticancer drugs often damage normal cells that, like cancer cells, are dividing rapidly. These include cells in the digestive system and in the roots of the hair, which is why people undergoing treatment with radiation or drugs often vomit and lose their hair. Cells in the immune system are also likely to be damaged, so these people may catch more infections than healthy people. Very often they become tired easily as well.

These unwanted actions, or side effects, sometimes make life miserable during cancer treatment. Most of them go away soon after treatment stops, however. Hair grows back within six to nine months, for example. Researchers have also developed ways to control many side effects. Drugs usually can stop nausea, and medicated creams can control the skin irritation that sometimes develops after radiation treatment.

Another way of reducing side effects is combining types of treatment. A person might receive radiation or chemotherapy after surgery, for instance. When treatments are combined, less of each can be used to get the same results. The chances of curing the cancer are also increased.

Surgery

Surgery is the oldest way to treat cancer. Until the second half of this century, it was just about the only way.

Surgeons used to remove large amounts of normal tissue around the tumors they took out in an attempt to make sure that no cancer cells would remain in the body. A person with cancer in a leg bone might lose the whole leg, for example. A woman with breast cancer usually would lose the whole breast. The surgeon would also remove the chest muscles on that side and the lymph nodes under the woman's arm, because breast cancer often spreads to these nodes.

Thanks to combination treatments, such major surgery often is no longer needed. For instance, if a small cancerous lump is found in a woman's breast, many surgeons now take out just the lump and a fairly small amount of surrounding tissue. After the woman recovers from the operation, she is given radiation and, sometimes, chemotherapy to kill

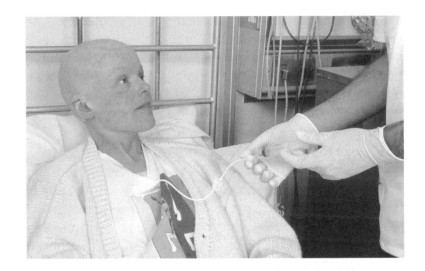

Radiation and anti-cancer drugs often damage healthy cells, causing hair loss and other unpleasant side effects.

any remaining cancer cells. Several studies have shown that women given such combined treatment are just as likely to be cured as women whose whole breast is removed.

Surgery can now be combined with other treatments to save the arms or legs of people with bone cancer, too. The surgeon cuts out only the tumor, and the missing piece of bone is replaced with a bone graft or a steel pin. The patient is given chemotherapy to kill any cancer cells remaining in the limb. If the cancer has not spread, chances are good that the disease will be cured, and the person will have normal or almost normal use of the limb.

Cutting out a tumor can often cure cancer completely if the disease has not spread. Even when a cure by surgery alone is not possible, removing a large tumor reduces the number of cancer cells in the body, which improves the chances that radiation or drug treatment will wipe out the remaining cells. It gives the patient a greater chance of at least having a remission. Removing a large tumor also stops pressure against nerves or other organs, which cuts down on pain and other problems.

Radiation

Radiation is a second, very common way to treat cancer. X rays and radiation from radioactive substances such as radium began to be used to treat cancer soon after their discovery at the end of the nineteenth century. At first they were used to treat only skin cancer and other cancers near the surface of the body. In the 1950s, however, doctors began to use new kinds of high-energy radiation, such as the gamma rays that come from radioactive cobalt. These rays can reach deep tumors.

Today, with the help of computerized imaging methods, doctors can direct radiation very precisely into tumors. They may send weak beams of radiation into a tumor from many angles, for example. Each beam harms only a small number of normal cells, but when the beams come together, they all destroy cells in the tumor.

Another treatment technique uses tiny, hollow tubes containing material that sends out radiation over a very short distance. Surgeons place the tubes in or near the tumor. In one version of this technique, a robotic arm guided by a computer implants radiation-containing tubes into brain tumors. Because the radiation cannot travel far, it harms few healthy cells.

Sometimes radiation can be used instead of destructive surgery. This works in some cases of cancer of the larynx, for instance. Formerly, many people with this kind of cancer had to have their larynx and vocal cords removed. After

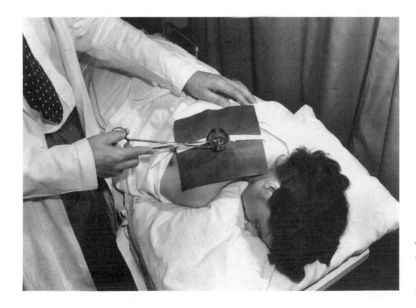

An applicator, placed over a tumor, gives off radiation that attacks the cancerous growth.

the surgery, they could speak only with a special device implanted in the throat. Today, some of these people can be treated with radiation alone, sparing their vocal cords and voices. Their chances of being cured of the cancer are just as good as with surgery.

Chemotherapy

Chemotherapy is the newest of the common forms of cancer treatment. Except for a few hormones, drugs have successfully treated cancer only since the late 1940s. Ironically, the first effective anticancer drug, nitrogen mustard, was derived from mustard gas, a toxic gas used in chemical warfare during World War I. After an accidental leak of a stockpile of the gas poisoned nearby soldiers during World War II, doctors treating them found that it had destroyed types of cells that are overproduced in certain blood cancers. Scientists began looking for a less deadly chemical relative that might be used to treat such cancers, and nitrogen mustard was the result.

Unlike radiation and surgery, anticancer drugs can spread all through the body, "mopping up" cells that have escaped from a tumor. Chemotherapy is often used after surgery or radiation treatment for this purpose. Drugs are also used alone to treat tumors in vital organs, where surgery is impractical, or to treat cancers that spread throughout the body, such as blood cell cancers.

More than fifty drugs are used against cancer today. Some are artificial compounds whose formulas were worked out on a computer. Others come from nature. Plants, ranging from common weeds to exotic rain forest dwellers, have yielded many substances that attack cancer cells. For instance, taxol, an anticancer drug developed in the early 1990s, was first made from a rare species of yew tree. (It is now made synthetically.)

Anticancer drugs attack tumors in several different ways. Some drugs tangle DNA strands, which prevents cell division. Others trick cancer cells into consuming the drugs instead of nutrients that the cells need, in effect starving the cancer cells to death. A third group boosts the immune sys-

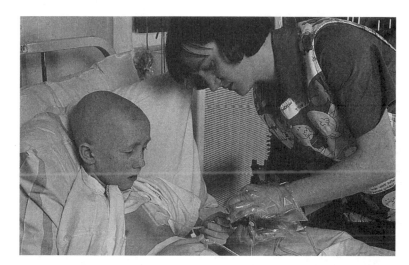

Hope for saving children with leukemia has grown over the last four decades.

tem's power to attack and destroy cancer cells. Scientists have recently learned that many chemotherapy drugs do not kill cancer cells directly but, instead, reactivate the built-in program that makes abnormal cells kill themselves.

A cancer patient often is treated with a combination of drugs, including drugs of several different types. This works better than treatment with a single drug because cancer cells often become resistant to one drug; however, another drug that attacks them in a different way may still be able to kill them. Combining drugs also means that fairly low doses of each kind can be used, which reduces side effects. Leading cancer researcher Mark Scolnick says, "When you are trying to kill cancer cells, you're always likely to need combination treatment."[25]

Chemotherapy has achieved some spectacular successes. In the 1950s, for example, a child with leukemia most often lived only a few months. Today, though, drug treatment can send most leukemic children into a remission that lasts for years. About half of the children who get leukemia today can be cured completely.

Problems remain, however. Most of the "miracle cures" have been for cancers that affect young people or are fairly rare. The most common kinds of cancer, such as cancers of the lung, colon, and breast, occur in older people and are still very hard to cure unless caught early.

Alternative treatments

Some people think that the standard treatments for cancer are both too ineffective and too toxic. This has resulted in the development of other kinds of treatments. Because these treatments differ from the ones that most doctors use, they are collectively called alternative treatments or therapies.

Alternative treatments fall into several groups. One large group focuses on diet. Practitioners of these therapies often tell people to eat only fruits, vegetables, and grains raised without pesticides or other artificial chemicals, and sometimes certain dairy products. They believe that other foods contain toxic substances that contribute to cancer. They may supplement this diet with vitamins, nutrients such as amino acids, herbs, or more exotic substances such as shark cartilage.

Another group of alternative treatments teaches people to use their minds to attack their cancer. For instance, practitioners may tell people to imagine their immune cells killing their tumor cells as knights in old stories slew dragons. Other therapies in this group use hypnosis or teach people mental exercises, such as biofeedback or meditation techniques, to control pain or fight depression. Still others call on religious belief and prayer.

A third group of alternative therapies uses physical treatments. Some of these, such as reflexology (which massages different spots on the foot to clear "energy channels" in the body) and acupressure (acupuncture without needles), are borrowed from other cultures.

Helpers or frauds?

An increasing number of both cancer patients and mainstream doctors feel that some alternative therapies can be useful. At the very least, such treatments usually make people feel better. They can help patients feel more in control of their disease and their treatment, provide attention and emotional support, and offer hope that helps to fight the depression a serious illness is likely to bring.

Some alternative treatments may have medical value as well. Some evidence suggests that the mind can affect disease by acting through the immune system, so a change in attitude or belief may well have an effect on health. Chemotherapy expert I. Craig Henderson says, "There is better evidence right now that group therapy extends survival time [of women] with breast cancer than there is similar evidence for bone marrow transplantation [a risky, 'last ditch' form of standard therapy given to some patients with advanced cancer]."[26]

More patients—some studies say half or more of all cancer patients—are demanding alternative therapies, and some hospitals and medical centers, such as Duke Comprehensive Cancer Center in Durham, North Carolina, make some of these treatments available in addition to standard ones. "We're comfortable with it as long as patients understand that it's not going to cure their cancer in and of itself," said O. Michael Colvin, director of the center in 1996. "It's . . . designed . . . to help patients deal with the stress of cancer and conventional treatments."[27] Such centers often refer to alternative treatments as "complementary care." Research has convinced regulatory agencies that these therapies are completely ineffective or even harmful, however, and these treatments are therefore banned in the United States.

Combined with traditional anticancer treatments, alternative treatments may be helpful.

Evaluating alternative treatments

Arguments continue to rage over alternative treatments. Alternative practitioners often say that conventional doctors and research scientists are too narrow-minded or too closely allied with the drug-producing industry to consider unconventional ideas. The doctors and scientists respond by

saying that most alternative practitioners provide little or no scientific evidence to support claims for their treatments.

Evidence for the effectiveness of some alternative treatments is better than for others. Studies that involve large numbers of people and are carried out according to accepted scientific procedures provide the best evidence. Many practitioners of alternative medicine, however, base their claims mainly on reports from people (sometimes including the practitioners themselves) who say that the treatments have cured them of cancer. Scientists warn that even if someone genuinely believes that a certain treatment cured him or her, the belief may not be correct. The cure may have resulted from another factor or may have happened without treatment. The person may never even have had cancer.

Most doctors stress that if people with cancer want to try alternative treatments, they should do so in addition to regular anticancer treatments, not in place of them. Doctors admit that surgery, radiation, and chemotherapy are far from perfect, but most feel that, at least for now, these are still the best weapons against cancer.

7

Will Researchers
Soon Cure Cancer?

"TEST DRUGS SHOWN to Eradicate Cancer" proclaimed a headline on May 3, 1998. The first paragraph of the story beneath claimed that two new drugs could "eradicate any type of cancer, with no obvious side effects and no drug resistance." But then came the catch: "in mice."[28]

Many scientists— and ordinary people, too, especially people with cancer and their loved ones—are thrilled by headlines like this, which appear every few years. Many others, however, sigh and say that they have seen it all before, and little or nothing changed as a result. Both groups are right: There is good reason for excitement about drugs like the ones described in the news story, but many earlier treatments greeted with equal excitement have proved to be failures when tested further.

Breakthrough or false hope?

Drugs like the one in the May 1998 story promise more hope than ever before because they represent new approaches to cancer treatment. "Traditional anticancer agents have been discovered through chance. We are now going after the fundamental mechanisms of cancer,"[29] says Allen Oliff, chief cancer researcher of the drug company Merck.

The new treatments are based solidly on the discoveries that researchers have made in the last twenty years about the changes in genes and cell chemicals that lie at the root of cancer. Instead of trying to kill cancer cells, these treatments either help the immune system do the job or trick the cells into killing themselves. Some treatments slow the cells' growth or even "rehabilitate" them so that they once again become normal. The new treatments should be both more effective and less harmful to normal cells than the standard cancer treatments of today.

Nonetheless, the fact that a treatment makes good scientific sense, or even that it works in animals, is no guarantee that it will help humans. Other new cancer treatments were announced with equally blaring headlines in the 1980s and early 1990s, only to prove useless, too toxic, or effective only on one or two types of cancer. James Pluda, who oversees research on anticancer compounds for the investigational drug branch of the National Cancer Institute, said a few days after the "eradicate cancer" headline appeared, "We have to remember that the field of [cancer research] . . . is littered with the bodies of therapeutic agents [treatments] that were going to be the next cure."[30]

Cutting off cancer's blood supply

The approach behind angiostatin and endostatin, the drugs that made the May 1998 headlines, is not really new at all. Judah Folkman of Children's Hospital in Boston, the scientist in whose laboratory the two compounds were dis-

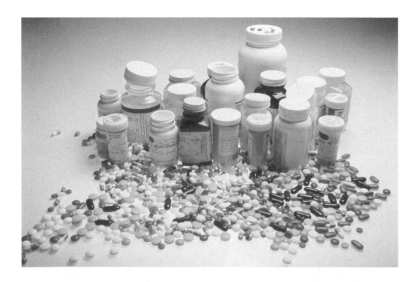

Breakthroughs in drug research offer hope for cancer patients.

covered, had been pursuing this approach for more than thirty-five years before his work hit the news. During the first part of that time, most other researchers greeted his ideas with "hostility and ridicule,"[31] Folkman told *Newsweek*.

Around 1960, Folkman began to think about the fact that cancers have a special power: They can create their own blood supply. New blood vessels normally grow in adults only during pregnancy or in healing wounds. Tumors, however, can somehow attract blood vessels and make the vessels continue growing inside them, a process called angiogenesis.

Researcher Judah Folkman has found substances that inhibit blood vessel growth in cancers.

This power also represents a potential weakness. The tumors depend on their blood supply to bring oxygen and nutrients to their interiors, and without it they can grow no larger than a pea. They also cannot spread, because blood vessels are the highways that carry cancer cells to distant parts of the body. Folkman reasoned that if he could block angiogenesis, cancers might remain too small to become a threat to health.

Over the years, Folkman and his coworkers found a number of substances that inhibited blood vessel growth, but most of the compounds' anticancer effects were weak. In the early 1990s, however, they thought of looking for inhibitors in what might seem a strange place: tumors themselves. Some cancer specialists had noticed that, after a large tumor was removed by surgery, smaller tumors nearby sometimes began to grow. This fact made Folkman suspect that the large tumor had been sending out some substance that limited the growth of the smaller ones, perhaps by keeping them from creating a blood supply. Michael O'Reilly, a member of Folkman's laboratory, found tiny amounts of an angiogenesis-inhibiting substance in the urine of cancer-bearing mice in 1994 and named it angiostatin. Two years later, he found a second inhibitor, which he called endostatin.

No matter how well angiostatin and endostatin work in mice, scientists estimate that it will take at least ten years of testing to establish its safety and effectiveness in humans.

A long road of testing

Once they had found angiostatin and endostatin, Folkman and his coworkers did what is usually done with promising anticancer drugs: They tested them on mice. They found that the two compounds, used together, destroyed three different types of large human tumors grafted onto the animals. "There was no tumor left—we couldn't even find it with a microscope,"[32] Folkman said. This was the research that produced the newspaper headlines.

The front-page *New York Times* article that broke the story quoted Richard Klausner, head of the National Cancer Institute, as saying that the new drugs were "the single most exciting thing on the horizon"[33] for treating cancer. Still, as Folkman and many other scientists pointed out, success in treating mice does not guarantee success in people. "If curing mice cancers were enough, we would have cured cancer in the '60s,"[34] said Donald Morton of the John Wayne Cancer Institute. Only 10 to 20 percent of substances that destroy cancers in mice prove to be useful for treating humans.

No matter how well angiostatin and endostatin work in mice, at least ten more years of testing, costing as much as $400 million, is likely to be required to establish their safety and effectiveness in humans. In the United States, any proposed new medical treatment that has succeeded in animals must pass through three stages of human testing before it can be sold to the public. The first stage, Phase I, establishes the treatment's safety. In Phase II, the treatment is tried on a small number of people with advanced disease that has resisted all other treatments. If the treatment helps a certain number of these people, it is tried on a larger number of patients, and its effect is compared with that of a known treatment. Neither the patients nor the doctors involved in this Phase III testing know which treatment a particular patient is receiving until the test is over.

The U.S. Food and Drug Administration (FDA) approves a treatment for general use only after it has passed all these tests and more. Most other industrialized countries have similar agencies and testing procedures. In 1996 the FDA streamlined testing requirements for drugs used to treat life-threatening illnesses, including cancer, but gaining FDA approval is still a long, slow, costly process. Human testing of angiostatin and endostatin was expected to begin in early 1999.

Angiostatin and endostatin have been successful in reducing cancer tumors to the point that they cannot be detected by microscope.

400 mm³ Lewis Lung carcinoma

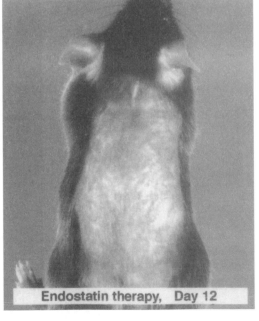

Endostatin therapy, Day 12

Angiostatin and endostatin are not the only reason that cancer researchers are excited today. They are just two of about a dozen angiogenesis inhibitors currently being tested in animals or humans. Furthermore, blocking the growth of blood vessels is only one of several novel approaches against cancer that has recently produced promising results.

Telomeres

Another approach, like angiogenesis inhibition, focuses on an important way in which cancer cells differ from normal ones. This difference involves bodies called telomeres, which appear on the ends of chromosomes. Each human cell has ninety-two telomeres, two for every chromosome. A telomere is a short sequence of "nonsense" DNA (DNA that does not provide information on which cells can act), repeated many times. The tips of chromosomes cannot be copied when the chromosomes reproduce

"Great news, guys! It looks like they've found a cure for cancer!"

themselves during cell division, but because these tips are telomeres, no important genetic information is lost. Instead, the telomeres simply grow a bit shorter each time the cell divides. Thus the telomeres protect the chromosomes, somewhat as the plastic tips on shoelaces keep the laces from unraveling.

Human cells start out with about a thousand DNA sequences in their telomeres, and they lose ten or twenty of them in each division. After fifty to a hundred divisions, the telomeres are used up. When this happens, the cells stop dividing and soon die, just as a burning candle goes out when its wick is used up. Cancer cells, however, contain an unusual chemical called telomerase, which can rebuild the telomeres. Because the cells never run out of telomeres, they potentially can go on dividing forever. They are deathless, or immortal.

Killing "immortal" cells

In humans, the only normal tissues that produce telomerase regularly are the ovaries and testes, which make sex cells during much of an adult's life, and a few other tissues such as blood, skin, and intestine, which constantly make more cells to renew themselves. A drug that blocks telomerase, therefore, should destroy cancer cells without harming most normal cells.

Blocking telomerase has killed cancer cells in the laboratory. Recent studies have shown, however, that mice lacking telomerase can develop tumors, which led Ronald DePinho of Albert Einstein College of Medicine in New York to say in 1997 that telomerase inhibition "may not be the phenomenal approach that we all hoped and prayed for."[35] Whether or not telomerase inhibition proves to be a useful cancer treatment, a test for telomerase may turn out to be useful for spotting some kinds of cancer.

The "smart bombs" that failed

Another hopeful approach uses immune substances called antibodies. When a bacterium, virus, or other foreign material enters the body, the immune system makes antibodies that attach to the surface of the material. A different type of antibody is produced for each kind of substance, called an antigen, on the surface of the invader. When an antibody attaches to its matching antigen, it signals immune system cells to attack the material bearing the antigen.

When a complex material such as ground-up cancer cells is injected into an animal, the animal's immune system produces hundreds of different kinds of antibodies. Until about twenty-five years ago, it was not possible to make a single type of antibody in large quantities. In 1975, however, two researchers in England, Cesar Milstein and Georg Kohler, developed a way to combine antibody-making cells with cells from a mouse cancer. Each of these blended cells grew into a tumorlike mass. All the cells in each mass were exact genetic copies, or clones, of each other, and all made exactly the same kind of antibody. Using Milstein and Kohler's technique, researchers could make as much of any particular antibody as they wished. Antibodies made in this way are called monoclonal ("one clone") antibodies.

Scientists in the 1980s were very excited about the possibility of using monoclonal antibodies to diagnose or treat cancer. They expected that, when monoclonal antibodies made to fit an antigen on cancer cells were injected into a person's body, the antibodies would home in on cells with that antigen anywhere in the body, like a "smart bomb" seeking its target. If weakly radioactive molecules were attached to the antibodies, the antibodies could let doctors diagnose cancer by scanning a person's body with an imaging device that picked up radiation. If molecules of a poison or a substance that gave off powerful, short-range radiation were attached instead, the antibodies would take their deadly cargo straight to the cancer, bypassing normal cells. Unfortunately, monoclonal antibodies were one of the "breakthrough" cancer discoveries that did not live up to their early promise. For one thing, because they came from mouse cells, the antibodies often triggered such a strong reaction from patients' immune systems that they could be given only once.

Improved antibodies

Recently, the technology of monoclonal antibodies has been improved, and interest in using them as a cancer treatment has revived. For instance, some antibodies are now made with mouse cells into which some human genes have been inserted, which reduces immune reactions against them. "Monoclonal antibodies were always a fantastic idea," says Mark Kaminski, a University of Michigan cancer researcher. "But because we didn't see the results we had hoped for, enthusiasm waned [died down]. Now it's time to start believing again."[36]

Dr. Dennis Slamon's research has led to a new cancer drug.

One type of monoclonal antibody, called Rituximab or Rituxan, was approved by the FDA in late 1997 for use against one type of lymphoma. It is the first monoclonal antibody to gain full FDA approval. It shrank tumors for up to a year in about half the patients tested and had fewer side effects than standard chemotherapy.

Another monoclonal antibody, to be marketed under the name Herceptin, attacks the protein produced by an oncogene called HER2/ncu. Cells in about 30 percent of breast cancers, including some of the cancers that are the fastest growing and hardest to treat, have extra copies of this gene and thus make extra protein. Like Rituximab, Herceptin is a last-ditch treatment for people with one type of advanced cancer. It does not cure the disease, but it extends life expectancy. Herceptin was approved by a panel of cancer experts that advises the FDA in September 1998 and seemed likely to gain full FDA approval by the end of the year.

Attacking cancer genes

Herceptin is the first anticancer drug designed from the beginning to block the product of an abnormal gene. It is also one of the first to attack a particular molecule within cells rather than trying to kill the cells themselves. Other experimental cancer treatments, not involving antibodies, also take this approach.

Still other new treatments focus on cancer-related genes themselves. For example, researchers are trying two different tactics aimed at p53, the tumor-suppressor gene that is missing or damaged in so many cancers. Both are based on the fact that adenoviruses, the kind of viruses that cause colds, must disable this gene before they can infect cells. In one approach, adenoviruses are changed by genetic engineering so that they cannot disable the gene. They thus can infect and kill only cells in which it is already missing—that is, cancer cells. The modified virus, which must be injected directly into tumors, was undergoing its first human testing in late 1997.

In an even more daring approach, researchers have made adenoviruses unable to kill cells and then inserted healthy p53 genes into the viruses. Instead of killing cancer cells, the viruses will carry a normal p53 gene into them. The gene, in turn, will either make the cells kill themselves immediately or restore the power of chemotherapy drugs to trigger such cell death. In mid-1998, versions of this treatment were in Phase II human testing.

Hope for the future

The new treatments described in this chapter are just a few of many now being tested. Any of them may become a powerful weapon against human cancer—or all of them, or none. Only time and testing will tell.

Time and testing have dashed many hopes in the past. Still, many researchers, including some of the most famous pioneers of cancer genetics, are cautiously optimistic that these or other approaches, probably used along with the traditional ones, will eventually provide cures, or at least greatly improved treatments, for many cancers. "As researchers, we feel a tremendous amount of hope, probably for the first time in the history of cancer treatment,"[37] says Bert Vogelstein of Johns Hopkins. Similarly, Nobel prizewinner Michael Bishop says, "For the first time in my life, I believe we will eventually be able to conquer cancer."[38]

Conclusion

HEALTH OFFICIALS ANNOUNCED in March 1998 that, for the first time in nearly twenty years, the number of cases of all cancers combined, and of most of the leading types of cancer as well, had declined in the United States. The incidence (rate of occurrence) of all cancers had increased an average of 1.2 percent per year between 1973 and 1990, but it decreased an average of 0.7 percent yearly between 1990 and 1995.

Death rates from cancer are also decreasing. Overall death rates rose an average of 0.4 percent per year between 1973 and 1990 but dropped an average of 0.5 percent thereafter. Officials believe that the declines result from a mixture of prevention through lifestyle changes such as decreases in smoking, earlier detection through screening tests, and improvements in treatment.

Will there ever be a cure?

Does this good news, coupled with the reports of "breakthrough" treatments now undergoing testing, mean that cancer will be cured in the next five or ten years? Most scientists think not. Many researchers are optimistic that new treatments will bring major improvements in cancer management, but most doubt that there will ever be a "magic bullet" for the disease—a drug or other treatment that destroys all types of cancers with little or no effect on normal cells. "There will never be a single cure for cancer,"[39] says the National Cancer Institute's Richard Klausner. Instead, cancer pioneer Robert Weinberg believes, "there will be

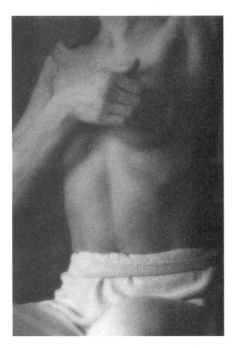

Cancer rates have decreased due to lifestyle changes, earlier detection, and improvements in treatment.

dozens [of cures], each tailor-made to a different kind of cancer, each informed [shaped] by one or another molecular peculiarity of the cancer cell."[40]

Even without any additional treatment breakthroughs, advocates say that cancer survival rates could improve further if treaments currently under investigation were tested more quickly and efficiently and then provided sooner to cancer clinics around the country. "We could reduce cancer mortality by 50 percent if we just got what we already know out to the patient,"[41] Ellen Stovall, executive director of the National Coalition for Cancer Survivorship, said in 1995.

An important part of getting the newest and best cancer treatments out to all patients is finding a way around the financial barriers that often block poor and minority people's access to health care. Harold Freeman, a cancer surgeon at Harlem Hospital Center in New York, estimates that if all Americans had access to tests that can detect cancer in its early stage, the survival rate for the disease would go from 50 percent to 75 percent.

Control and prevention

Some researchers believe that, in the future, the focus of research and treatment will change from curing cancer to controlling it. People diagnosed with cancer will take regular doses of angiogenesis inhibitors or other treatments all their lives to keep their tumors small and harmless, much as people with diabetes now control their illness by modifying their diet and taking daily insulin injections or pills. Cancer will thus change from a virtual death sentence to a chronic (permanent) but survivable disease, much like what is starting to happen with AIDS. Lance Liotta of the National Cancer Institute says, "We don't cure diseases like diabetes and hypertension [high blood pressure]. We control them. Why can't we look at cancer this way?"[42]

Some people, such as John Bailar, chairman of health studies at the University of Chicago, would like to see a different shift in priorities for cancer research. "I'm convinced that a major emphasis in cancer research should be shifted from cancer treatment to cancer prevention,"[43] Bailar told a Senate subcommittee in 1997. He urged that the proportion of the National Cancer Institute budget devoted to research on prevention be increased from its present one-fourth to two-thirds. Bailar and those who agree with him feel that preventing cancer, whether by removing carcinogens from the environment or by urging people to make lifestyle changes that reduce cancer risk, will prove more effective than trying to treat or control the disease once it has developed.

In the meantime, even though cancer research has not produced a "magic bullet" and may never do so, it has certainly not been a failure. In addition to producing a detailed understanding of and improving treatments for a deadly disease, it has provided invaluable knowledge about how cells grow, reproduce, and carry out their activities. It has shed new light on the incredibly complex interaction of genes and molecules that forms the basis of all life.

Some researchers believe the emphasis on curing cancer will change to controlling it—much as diabetics control their disease with insulin injections and healthy diet.

Notes

Introduction

1. Quoted in Barbara Mantel, "Advances in Cancer Research," *CQ Researcher Summary*, August 25, 1995, p. 1.
2. Quoted in Jean Marx, "Oncogenes Reach a Milestone," *Science*, December 23, 1994, p. 1942.

Chapter 1: What Is Cancer?

3. Quoted in Rita Rubin, "The War on Cancer," *U.S. News & World Report*, February 5, 1996, p. 56.
4. Quoted in J. Madeleine Nash, "Stopping Cancer in Its Tracks," *Time*, April 25, 1994, p. 58.

Chapter 2: What Causes Cancer?

5. Quoted in Natalie Angier, *Natural Obsessions*. New York: Warner Books, 1989, p. 67.
6. Quoted in Robert F. Service, "Stalking the Start of Colon Cancer," *Science*, March 18, 1994, p. 1559.
7. Quoted in Michael Waldholz, *Curing Cancer*. New York: Simon & Schuster, 1997, p. 278.

Chapter 3: What Raises Cancer Risk?

8. Quoted in Mike Weilbacher, "Toxic Shock," *E*, June 1995.
9. Quoted in Weilbacher, "Toxic Shock."
10. Quoted in Doug Hamilton, "Interview with Theo Colborn," *Frontline Online*, July 22, 1998. Available at www.pbs.org/wgbh/pages/frontline/shows/nature/interviews/colborn.html.
11. Elizabeth M. Whelan, "Stop Banning Products at the Drop of a Rat," *Insight on the News*, December 12, 1994, p. 19.

12. Quoted in Weilbacher, "Toxic Shock."

13. Quoted in Weilbacher, "Toxic Shock."

14. Quoted in Doug Hamilton, "Interview with Linda Birnbaum," *Frontline Online*, July 22, 1998. Available at www.pbs.org/wgbh/pages/frontline/shows/nature/interviews/birnbaum.html.

15. Quoted in Warren E. Leary, "Scientists See No Risk in EMFs," *San Francisco Chronicle* (from the *New York Times*), November 1, 1996, p. A23.

16. Quoted in Hamilton, "Interview with Linda Birnbaum."

17. Quoted in Weilbacher, "Toxic Shock."

18. Quoted in Hamilton, "Interview with Theo Colborn."

Chapter 4: How Can Cancer Be Prevented?

19. Robert N. Proctor, "No Time for Heroes," *Sciences*, March/April 1995.

20. Quoted in Patricia Hittner, "Seven Cancer Fighters That *Really* Work," *Better Homes and Gardens*, July 1995, p. 52.

21. Quoted in Rita Rubin, "Do You Have a Cancer Gene?" *U.S. News & World Report*, May 13, 1996, p. 74.

22. Quoted in Janet Raloff, "Drug Prevents Some Cancer, Poses Risks," *Science News*, April 11, 1998, p. 228.

23. R. Grant Steen, "Winning the War on Cancer," *Futurist*, March/April 1997, p. 28.

24. Proctor, "No Time for Heroes."

Chapter 6: How Is Cancer Treated?

25. Quoted in Christine Gorman, "The Hope and the Hype," *Time*, May 18, 1998, p. 50.

26. Quoted in Henry Dreher, "Cancer and the Politics of Meaning," *Tikkun*, January/February 1998, p. 17.

27. Quoted in Doug Podolsky, "A New Age of Healing Hands," *U.S. News & World Report*, February 5, 1996, p. 71.

Chapter 7: Will Researchers Soon Cure Cancer?

28. Gina Kolata, "Test Drugs Shown to Eradicate Cancer," *San Francisco Chronicle* (from the *New York Times*), May 3, 1998, p. 1.

29. Quoted in Robert Langreth, "Arsenal of Hope," *Wall Street Journal*, May 6, 1998, p. A12.

30. Quoted in "More Cold Water Dampens Hopes for New Cancer Drugs," *San Francisco Chronicle*, May 6, 1998, p. A13.

31. Quoted in Shannon Begley and Claudia Kalb, "One Man's Quest to Cure Cancer," *Newsweek*, May 18, 1998, p. 56.

32. Quoted in Kolata, "Test Drugs Shown to Eradicate Cancer," p. 20.

33. Quoted in Kolata, "Test Drugs Shown to Eradicate Cancer," p. 1.

34. Quoted in Begley and Kalb, "One Man's Quest to Cure Cancer," p. 61.

35. Quoted in John Travis, "Missing Enzyme Incites Cancer Debate," *Science News*, October 11, 1997, p. 228.

36. Quoted in J. Madeleine Nash, "The Enemy Within," *Time*, Fall 1996.

37. Quoted in Gorman, "The Hope and the Hype," p. 47.

38. Quoted in Langreth, "Arsenal of Hope," p. A1.

Conclusion

39. Quoted in Nash, "The Enemy Within."

40. Robert A. Weinberg, *Racing to the Beginning of the Road*. New York: Harmony Books, 1996, p. 262.

41. Quoted in Mantel, "Advances in Cancer Research," p. 2.

42. Quoted in Nash, "Stopping Cancer in Its Tracks," p. 61.

43. Quoted in Samuel Epstein, "Winning the War Against Cancer? . . . Are They Even Fighting It?" *Ecologist*, March/April 1998.

Glossary

---

acupressure: A Chinese method of treating illness by massaging certain points on the body (the same points used in acupuncture).

adenovirus: A type of virus that causes colds; in modified form, it may be used in the future to treat some kinds of cancer.

alternative treatments or therapies: Treatments for illness that are different from the ones used by most doctors.

angiogenesis: The process by which a cancerous tumor causes new blood vessels to grow inside itself to provide it with nutrients.

angiostatin: An experimental anticancer drug that prevents blood vessel growth in tumors.

antibody: A substance made by certain immune system cells that attaches to a particular antigen and marks the bearer of the antigen for destruction by the immune system.

antigen: A substance on the surface of a cell, virus, or other substance that acts as a marker for the immune system.

base: One of four substances in DNA; the order of bases in a DNA molecule "spells out" the information in genes.

benign: Not cancerous.

biofeedback: A mental exercise that allows people to control body functions such as blood pressure and response to pain.

biopsy: A small sample of tissue taken from a tumor or part of the body for medical examination.

bone marrow: The fatty material inside some bones, where all blood cells are made.

bronchial tubes: The tubes through which air moves in and out of the lungs.

bronchoscope: A tube through which a doctor can look into the bronchial tubes and, if necessary, remove a small tissue sample.

cancer: A group of diseases in which some cells of the body grow without stopping and invade other tissue.

carcinogen: A factor in the environment that increases the risk of getting cancer.

carcinoma: A cancer made from cells that come from the linings of the body.

cells: The microscopic units of which the bodies of all living things are made.

cervix: The neck of the uterus or womb.

chemotherapy: Treatment of cancer or other diseases by drugs.

chromosomes: Worm-shaped structures, made primarily of DNA, that contain the genetic material of a cell.

chronic: Long-lasting or permanent.

clone: A cell or living thing that has exactly the same genes as another cell or living thing; a genetic copy.

colon: Part of the large intestine.

CT scan (CAT scan, computerized axial tomography): An X-ray picture, made from many images combined by a computer, that shows a cross section of the body.

culture: A group of cells grown in a laboratory dish.

detection test: Test done on people who have symptoms of a disease to determine the nature and extent of the disease.

diagnose: Detect, find out the nature of.

DNA: Deoxyribonucleic acid, the chemical of which genes are made.

electromagnetic field (EMF): The sphere-shaped area filled by energy that spreads out around a device that carries or uses electricity.

endoscope: A tube containing light-transmitting fibers that is inserted into a body opening to allow a doctor to examine hollow organs inside the body.

endostatin: An experimental anticancer drug that prevents blood vessel growth in tumors.

Environmental Protection Agency (EPA): A federal government agency responsible for protecting Americans and their environment against harmful substances.

epidemiologist: Scientist who tries to find out which living things get certain diseases and how they differ from those that do not develop those diseases.

epidemiology: The study of factors contributing to the occurrence and spread of disease.

esophagus: The tube leading from the throat to the stomach.

estrogen: A female hormone.

fetus: A living thing in the later stages of development before birth.

fiber: Indigestible plant matter.

Food and Drug Administration (FDA): A federal government agency chiefly responsible for protecting Americans against harmful or ineffective medical treatments and against harmful substances in food.

gamma rays: A form of high-energy radiation sometimes used to treat cancer.

gene: The part of a DNA molecule that contains instructions for making a protein or part of one; the unit of a cell's inherited information.

genome: A cell's complete collection of genes.

hemoglobin: A pigment in red blood cells that carries oxygen.

Herceptin: A monoclonal antibody that blocks the protein made by the oncogene HER2/neu, an experimental treatment for breast cancer.

hormone: A natural substance that carries chemical messages from one part of the body to another.

immune system: The body system, consisting of certain cells and chemicals in the blood and lymph, that protects against foreign microorganisms or substances.

inherited: Passed on through genes received from parents.

larynx: Voice box.

leukemia: One of several types of cancer in which too many white blood cells are produced.

lymph: A milky fluid carried through the body in vessels, separate from but connected to the blood vessel system.

lymph nodes: Small organs that make and store lymph cells; they are part of the immune system.

lymphoma: One of several types of cancer in which too many lymph cells are produced.

magnetic resonance imaging (MRI): A way of detecting disease in which changes in atoms caused by a strong magnetic field are used to make three-dimensional pictures of the body.

malignant: Cancerous.

mammogram: An X-ray picture of the breast.

mammography: An X-ray screening test for breast cancer.

melanoma: A dangerous, fast-growing form of skin cancer that begins in cells containing a dark pigment called melanin.

metastasis: A secondary cancerous tumor formed from a cell or cells that escaped from an earlier tumor in another part of the body; the power of cancer cells to spread from one part of the body to another.

metastasize: Spread to a distant part of the body.

monoclonal antibodies: Identical antibodies, all reacting to the same antigen, produced by cloned cells in the laboratory.

mucus: A thick, slimy body fluid.

mutation: Change in a gene.

nitrogen mustard: The first chemical, other than hormones, to successfully treat a human cancer; a relative of mustard gas.

nucleus: The central body of a cell, which contains the cell's chromosomes and genes.

obese: Greatly overweight; more than 20 percent over ideal body weight.

oncogene: A normal cell gene that can cause cancer if it is mutated or moved.

oncologist: Doctor who specializes in treating cancer.

organ: A group of tissues that work together to do one job (e.g., liver, lung).

organochlorines: Complex compounds containing the elements carbon and chlorine that are used in many industrial processes and products; they can disrupt the action of hormones and are suspected of increasing cancer risk.

p53: A tumor-suppressor gene that is inactivated in many common cancers.

Pap test: Screening test for cancer of the cervix, named after its inventor, Dr. Papanicolau.

pathologist: Doctor who studies diseased tissue.

placebo: A pill or other treatment that has no medical effect.

polyp: A benign tumor of the colon that may later become cancerous.

prostate: A male reproductive organ that produces the fluid part of semen.

prostate-specific antigen (PSA) test: A detection test for prostate cancer.

protein: One of the many chemicals produced by genes that allow a cell to do its work.

radiation: Energy that spreads out from a source; sometimes short for "high-energy radiation," as in radiation treatment for cancer.

radioactivity: Ability to give off high-energy radiation.

radium: An element that gives off high-energy radiation naturally.

raloxifene: A drug that may prevent breast cancer without increasing the risk of uterine cancer.

ras: The first oncogene discovered to be involved in human cancer.

Rb: The tumor-suppressor gene that is missing or inactive in retinoblastoma and several other cancers.

red blood cells: Blood cells that carry oxygen through the body.

reflexology: A treatment for disease in which spots on the foot are massaged to clear energy channels in the body.

remission: Time following cancer treatment during which no cancer cells can be detected in the body.

retinoblastoma: A rare eye cancer that strikes young children and is caused by the absence of a tumor-suppressor gene.

Rituximab (Rituxan): The first monoclonal antibody approved by the FDA for cancer treatment; it treats one form of lymphoma.

sarcoma: A cancer made of cells that came from tissues that hold the body together.

screening test: A test done on apparently healthy people to detect disease before symptoms appear.

secondhand smoke: Cigarette smoke breathed in by nonsmokers near a smoker.

sex cells: Eggs (female) and sperm (male), the cells that combine to form a new living thing.

side effects: Undesirable effects of a medical treatment.

src: The first oncogene to be discovered.

symptom: A sign of disease in the body.

tamoxifen: A drug that helps to prevent breast cancer in women who have previously had the disease or are at high risk for it.

taxol: A drug, originally made from a type of yew tree, that is used to treat some forms of cancer.

telomerase: A substance, possessed primarily by cancer cells, that can rebuild telomeres and prevent cell aging and death.

telomere: A body on the end of a chromosome that protects genetic material from loss during cell reproduction.

tissue: A group of cells that do the same kind of job.

tumor: Mass of diseased cells, sometimes but not always cancerous.

tumor-suppressor gene: A gene that normally prevents cancerous growth; such genes are inactivated in many cancers.

ultraviolet light: An invisible, high-energy part of sunlight that can cause skin cancer.

uterus: The organ in which a woman carries an unborn baby.

white blood cells: Blood cells that are part of the immune system.

X rays: A form of high-energy radiation that can make images of the inside of the body and can either cause or detect cancer.

Organizations
to Contact

American Brain Tumor Association
2720 River Rd., Suite 146
Des Plaines, IL 60018-4110
(800) 886-2282
e-mail: info@abta.org
Internet: www.abta.org

This organization offers information and social support for people with brain tumors and their families.

American Cancer Society
1599 Clifton Rd. NE
Atlanta, GA 30329
(800) 227-2345
Internet: www.cancer.org

This large organization offers information about all aspects of cancer and related issues and supports research, prevention efforts, and patient services.

Cancer Care
1180 Avenue of the Americas
New York, NY 10036
(212) 221-3300
e-mail: info@cancercareinc.org
Internet: www.cancercareinc.org

Cancer Care offers free professional assistance to people with cancer, including publications and other information, counseling, referrals, and financial assistance.

Cancer Federation
PO Box 1298
Banning, CA 92220-0009
(909) 849-4325

The Cancer Federation offers publications, counseling, and other help for cancer patients, their families, and healing professionals.

The Candlelighters Childhood Cancer Foundation
7910 Woodmont Ave., Suite 460
Bethesda, MD 20814-3015
(800) 366-2223
e-mail: info@candlelighters.org
Internet: www.candlelighters.org

This organization offers information about childhood cancer and support for children with cancer and their families.

The Chemotherapy Foundation
183 Madison Ave., Suite 403
New York, NY 10016
(212) 213-9292

The Chemotherapy Foundation encourages research into the control, cure, and prevention of cancer through drugs, and it educates health professionals, cancer patients, and the public about chemotherapy.

Foundation for Advancement in Cancer Therapy
PO Box 1242, Old Chelsea Station
New York, NY 10113
(212) 741-2790

This organization educates cancer patients, their families, and the public about alternative treatments for cancer that it considers safe and nontoxic.

Leukemia Society of America
600 Third Ave.
New York, NY 10016
(212) 573-8484
Internet: www.leukemia.org

This organization offers information about various kinds of leukemia and their treatment.

National Alliance of Breast Cancer Organizations (NABCO)
9 E. 37th St., 10th Floor
New York, NY 10016
(888) 806-2226
e-mail: NABCOinfo@aol.com
Internet: www.nabco.org

The NABCO offers a resource list of publications about breast cancer.

National Cancer Institute
PO Box 24128
Baltimore, MD 21227
(800) 422-6237 (800-4-CANCER)
Internet: http://rex.nci.nih.gov and http://cancernet.nci.nih.gov

This government-sponsored organization, part of the National Institutes of Health, sponsors research on cancer and offers a wide variety of educational material about cancer.

Patient Advocates for Advanced Cancer Treatments (PAACT)
1143 Parmelee NW
Grand Rapids, MI 49504-3844
(616) 453-1477
e-mail: PCA@PCAPAACTINC.COM
Internet: www.osz.com/paact

PAACT offers educational material about prostate cancer and its treatment.

People Against Cancer
604 East St.
PO Box 10
Otho, Iowa 50569
(515) 972-4444
e-mail: nocancer@ix.netcom.com
Internet: www.dodgenet.com/nocancer

People Against Cancer offers information and counseling about alternative therapies for cancer.

The Skin Cancer Foundation
245 Fifth Ave., Suite 1403
New York, NY 10016
(212) 725-5176
e-mail: info@skincancer.org
Internet: www.skincancer.org

This foundation offers educational material about skin cancer and its prevention.

The Susan G. Komen Breast Cancer Foundation
5005 LBJ Freeway, Suite 370
Dallas, TX 75244
(972) 855-1600
e-mail: education@komen.org
Internet: www.breastcancerinfo.com and www.komen.org

This organization works to eradicate breast cancer through research, education, screening, and treatment and provides educational materials about breast cancer and breast care.

Y-Me National Breast Cancer Organization
c/o Susan Nathanson
212 W. Van Buren
Chicago, IL 60607-3908
(800) 221-2141
e-mail: help@y-me.org
Internet: www.y-me.org

This organization offers educational material about breast cancer in English and Spanish.

Suggestions for Further Reading

Books

Robert Buckman, *What You Really Need to Know About Cancer*. Baltimore, MD: Johns Hopkins University Press, 1997. Down-to-earth description of symptoms, tests, and treatments for different kinds of cancer as well as a general discussion of cancer, its causes, and how patients and their families can live with it.

Dean King, Jessica King, and Jonathan Pearlroth, *Cancer Combat*. New York: Bantam, 1998. Fascinating collection of accounts of and tips on dealing with cancer and cancer treatments by people who have survived the disease.

Robert N. Proctor, *Cancer Wars*. New York: BasicBooks, 1995. Discusses how politics affects (and often inhibits) cancer research, especially research into preventable environmental causes of cancer.

Michael Waldholz, *Curing Cancer*. New York: Simon & Schuster, 1997. Account of recent discoveries about the genetic changes that underlie cancer and the people who made them.

Periodicals

Mark Caldwell, "Beyond the Lab Rat," *Discover*, May 1996.

Christine Gorman, "The Hope and the Hype," *Time*, May 18, 1998.

Doug Podolsky, "A New Age of Healing Hands," *U.S. News & World Report*, February 5, 1996.

Rita Rubin, "Do You Have a Cancer Gene?" *U.S. News & World Report*, May 13, 1996.

R. Grant Steen, "Winning the War on Cancer," *Futurist*, March/April 1997.

Mike Weilbacher, "Toxic Shock," *E*, June 1995.

Works Consulted

Books

Natalie Angier, *Natural Obsessions*. New York: Warner Books, 1989. Fascinating account of the first discoveries of oncogenes and tumor-suppressor genes.

Gerald P. Murphy, Lois B. Morris, and Dianne Lange, *Informed Decisions*. New York: Viking, 1997. Book sponsored by the American Cancer Society that describes the nature of and treatments for different types of cancer and how to live with cancer.

Harold Varmus and Robert A. Weinberg, *Genes and the Biology of Cancer*. New York: Scientific American Library, 1993. Somewhat technical but well-illustrated account of the changes in genes and cell chemistry that underlie cancer.

Robert A. Weinberg, *Racing to the Beginning of the Road*. New York: Harmony Books, 1996. Account of the discoveries and personalities in one of the country's foremost cancer research laboratories during the 1970s and 1980s.

Periodicals

Lawrence K. Altman, "Drug Shown to Shrink Tumors in Type of Breast Cancer by Targeting Gene Defect," *New York Times*, May 18, 1998.

Marcia Barinaga, "From Bench Top to Bedside," *Science*, November 7, 1997.

Shannon Begley and Claudia Kalb, "One Man's Quest to Cure Cancer," *Newsweek*, May 18, 1998.

William J. Broad, "Physicists Pooh-Pooh Threat from Power Lines," *San Francisco Chronicle* (from the *New York Times*), May 14, 1995.

Henry Dreher, "Cancer and the Politics of Meaning," *Tikkun*, January/February 1998.

Tamara Eberlein, "Cancer Genes," *Redbook*, May 1995.

Samuel Epstein, "Winning the War Against Cancer? . . . Are They Even Fighting It?" *Ecologist*, March/April 1998.

Kathleen Fackelman, "Variations on a Theme," *Science News*, May 6, 1995.

Kristen Lidke Finn, "Breast Cancer: Alternatives to Mastectomy," *USA Today*, May 1995.

Stephen S. Hall, "Monoclonal Antibodies at Age 20: Promise at Last?" *Science*, November 10, 1995.

Doug Hamilton, "Interview with Linda Birnbaum," *Frontline Online*, July 22, 1998. Available at www.pbs.org/wgbh/pages/frontline/shows/nature/interviews/birnbaum.html.

———, "Interview with Theo Colborn," *Frontline Online*, July 22, 1998. Available at www.pbs.org/wgbh/pages/frontline/shows/nature/interviews/colborn.html.

Patricia Hittner, "Seven Cancer Fighters That *Really* Work," *Better Homes and Gardens*, July 1995.

"Inroads in the Battle Against Cancer," *Maclean's*, June 1, 1998.

Gina Kolata, "Mammogram Talks Prove Indefinite," *New York Times*, January 24, 1997.

———, "Test Drugs Shown to Eradicate Cancer," *San Francisco Chronicle* (from the *New York Times*), May 3, 1998.

Robert Langreth, "Arsenal of Hope," *Wall Street Journal*, May 6, 1998.

Walter Last, "The Diversity and Effectiveness of Natural Cancer Cures," *Ecologist*, March/April 1998.

Warren E. Leary, "Scientists See No Risk in EMFs," *San Francisco Chronicle* (from the *New York Times*), November 1, 1996.

Arthur M. Louis, "FDA OKs New Drug for Cancer," *San Francisco Chronicle*, November 27, 1997.

Barbara Mantel, "Advances in Cancer Research," *CQ Researcher Summary*, August 25, 1995.

Delia Marshall, "Mammograms Under 50?" *Working Woman*, October 1994.

Jean Marx, "Oncogenes Reach a Milestone," *Science*, December 23, 1994.

"More Cold Water Dampens Hopes for New Cancer Drugs," *San Francisco Chronicle*, May 6, 1998.

J. Madeleine Nash, "The Enemy Within," *Time*, Fall 1996.

———, "Stopping Cancer in Its Tracks," *Time*, April 25, 1994.

David Perlman, "2 New Breast Cancer Drugs OKd by FDA's Advisory Panel," *San Francisco Chronicle*, September 3, 1998.

Charles Petit, "Power Line Cancer Link Discounted," *San Francisco Chronicle*, July 3, 1997.

Robert N. Proctor, "No Time for Heroes," *Sciences*, March/April 1995.

Janet Raloff, "Drug Prevents Some Cancer, Poses Risks," *Science News*, April 11, 1998.

———, "EMFs' Biological Influences," *Science News*, January 10, 1998.

———, "Passive Smoking: Confirming the Risks," *Science News*, October 17, 1998.

Rita Rubin, "The War on Cancer," *U.S. News & World Report*, February 5, 1996.

Stephen Schwartz, "Electric Fields Linked to Leukemia," *San Francisco Chronicle*, October 1, 1998.

Robert F. Service, "Stalking the Start of Colon Cancer," *Science*, March 18, 1994.

"Stealth Surgery on Brain Tissue," *Science News*, August 26, 1995.

John Travis, "End Games," *Science News*, November 25, 1995.

————, "Missing Enzyme Incites Cancer Debate," *Science News*, October 11, 1997.

————, "New Test Spots Cancer Cells in Blood," *Science News*, April 18, 1998.

Elizabeth M. Whelan, "Stop Banning Products at the Drop of a Rat," *Insight on the News*, December 12, 1994.

Index

acupressure, as cancer
  treatment, 66
adenoviruses, in cancer
  therapy, 78
AIDS, 80
alcohol use
  cancer prevention and, 45
American Cancer
  Society, 52
  cancer warning signs
    listed by, 52
  recommendations of,
    for mammography, 55
American Medical Society
  recommendations of,
    for mammography, 55
angiogenesis, 71
  inhibitors, 80
angiostatin, 70, 71, 72
  testing of, 73
antibodies
  in cancer treatment,
    75–76
  in screening/detection
    tests, 58
antigens, 76

Bailar, John, 81
benign tumors, 12
biofeedback
  as cancer treatment, 66

biopsy, 58–59
  lung, 17
  skin, 18
Birnbaum, Linda, 39, 41
Bishop, Michael, 22, 23, 78
blood cells
  in leukemia, 19
bone cancer
  advances in treatment of,
    61–62
BRCA genes
  testing for, 46, 47
breast cancer, 15
  advances in treatment of,
    61–62
  age-specific probabilities of
    developing, 46
  alternative therapies for, 67
  antibody therapy for, 77
  genetic testing for, 45–46
  prevention of, 49
Broder, Samuel, 13

cancer
  cure of, 69–70, 78
    vs. control of, 80–81
  incidence of, 79
  kinds of, 11
  origin of word, 8
  screening tests for, 53–54
  spread of, 13–15

survival rates, 80
warning signs of, 52
see also prevention, risks,
  treatment
carcinogens
  mutations and, 29, 30
  testing of, 37–39
carcinomas, 14–15
cases, cancer, 9
CAT scan. *See* computerized
  axial tomography
  (CT scan)
cells
  control of, by genes, 21
  immortal
    killing of, 75
  normal behavior of, 11–12
  programmed death of, 13
Chassin, Mark, 34
chemotherapy, 64–65
  side effects of, 61
chromosomes, 25
cigarette smoke, 16, 20
  cancer deaths caused
    by, 43
  carcinogens in, 31
  secondhand, 43
Colborn, Theo, 34, 41
colon cancer, 15
  genetic changes leading
    to, 28
  obesity and, 45
  screening tests for, 54
Colvin, O. Michael, 67
computerized axial
  tomography (CT scan),
  17, 57
Curie, Marie, 32

deaths, cancer-related, 9, 79
  from lung cancer, 44
detection tests, 56
diet
  as cancer preventive, 44, 45
  as cancer treatment, 66
  as cause of cancer, 31
DNA (deoxyribonucleic
  acid), 21
  chemotherapy and, 64
  damage by carcinogens, 30
  errors in, 26–27
  nonsense, 74
DNA repair genes, 26–28

electromagnetic fields,
  low-intensity (EMF)
  as carcinogenic factor, 33,
    34–36, 41
endoscope, 59
endostatin, 70, 71, 72
  testing of, 73
Environmental Protection
  Agency (EPA), 37

Fisher, Bernard, 49
Folkman, Judah, 70, 71
food additives
  as potential carcinogens, 32
Food and Drug
  Administration (FDA), 37
  testing of anticancer drugs
    by, 73
Freeman, Harold, 80
Friend, Stephen H., 26

genes, 21
  cancer-related, hunt for, 29

tumor-suppressor, 26
genetic testing
  in cancer prevention, 45–46
  dangers of, 47–49

Henderson, I. Craig, 67
Herceptin, 77
HER2/neu oncogene, 77
Hippocrates, 8, 13
hormones
  disruption of, by EMFs, 36
  disruption of, by
    organochlorines, 33–34
hypnosis
  as cancer treatment, 66

immune system, 15
inheritance, genetic, 29

Kaminski, Mark, 77
Klausner, Richard, 11, 29,
  72, 79
Knudson, Alfred G., Jr.,
  24, 25
Kohler, Georg, 76

larynx cancer
  radiation therapy for, 63–64
Leder, Philip, 10
Leeper, Ed, 35
leukemias, 15–16, 19–20
  chemotherapy for, 65
lifestyle choices
  role in cancer, 31
lung cancer, 15, 16–17
  annual deaths from, 44
lymph
  spread of cancer by, 14

lymphomas, 16
  antibody therapy for, 77

magnetic resonance imaging
  (MRI), 57
  advantages of, 58
malignant tumors, 12
mammography, 54–55
melanoma, 14, 18, 19
metastases, 14
Milstein, Cesar, 76
monoclonal antibodies, 76
Morton, Donald, 72
MRI See magnetic
  resonance imaging (MRI)
Murray, F. Jay, 38
mutations, genetic, 22
  carcinogens and, 29, 30
  in tumor-related genes,
    27, 28

National Institute of
  Environmental Health
  Sciences
  on EMF risk, 36
National Research Council
  EMF research by, 36, 41
Newsweek, 71
New York Times, 72
nitrogen mustard, 64
Nixon, Richard, 8–9

obesity
  link with cancer, 44–45
Oliff, Allen, 69
oncogenes, discovery of, 22
O'Reilly, Michael, 71
organochlorines

as potential carcinogen,
33–34

Pap (Papanicolau) test,
53–54
pathologists, 17
pesticides
  as potential carcinogens, 32
  problems with banning
    of, 42
plastics
  as potential carcinogens, 32
prevention, cancer
  with diet, 44–45
  with drugs, 49–50
  genetic testing and, 45–46
    problems with, 47–49
  lifestyle choices and,
    43–44
  new stress on, 50–51
Proctor, Robert, 9, 51
prostate-specific antigen, 55

radiation
  as carcinogen, 31
  as treatment, 62–64
raloxifene, 50
ras gene
  antibody tests for, 58
  in colon cancer, 28
  link with human cancer, 23
Rb gene, 25
reflexology
  as cancer treatment, 66
retinoblastoma, 24
risks, cancer
  environmental sources of,
    30–31, 32–36

costs of eliminating,
    40–42
  by site and gender, 15
Rituximab/Rituxan, 77

sarcomas, 15
Scolnick, Mark, 65
screening tests
  for colon cancer, 54
  for prostate cancer, 55–56
  for uterine cancer, 53–54
secondhand smoke
  and cancer risk, 31, 43
skin cancer, 18–19
src gene, 22, 23
Stearns, Cliff, 49
Steen, R. Grant, 51
Stevens, Charles, 41
Stovall, Ellen, 80
sunlight
  protection from, 43
  ultraviolet rays in, 32
symptoms
  of leukemia, 19
  of lung cancer, 17
  of skin cancer, 18

tamoxifen, 49
  risks of, 49–50
taxol, 64
telomerase, 75
telomeres, 74–75
Thibault, Marie-Josee, 43
treatment, cancer
  alternative therapies, 66–68
  chemotherapy, 64–65
  in history, 8
  progress in, 60

radiation, 62–64
side effects of, 60–61
tumors
benign vs. malignant, 12
types of
carcinomas, 14–15
leukemias, 15–16
lymphomas, 16
sarcomas, 15
tumor-suppressor genes, 26
in colon cancer, 28
as targets of cancer
therapy, 78

ultraviolet rays
skin cancer and, 18

Varmus, Harold, 22, 23
viruses, 22
Vogelstein, Bert, 26, 28, 78

"war on cancer," 9
Weinberg, Robert, 26
Wertheimer, Nancy, 35, 41
Whelan, Elizabeth, 38, 41

Yunia, Jorge, 25

Picture Credits

About the Author

Lisa Yount earned a bachelor's degree with honors in English and creative writing from Stanford University. She has a lifelong interest in biology and medicine. She has been a professional writer for more than thirty years, producing educational materials, magazine articles, and over twenty books for young people. Several of her books have been placed on the New York Public Library's recommended list of Books for the Teen Age. Her books for Lucent include *Memory, Issues in Biomedical Ethics*, and (with Harry Henderson) *Twentieth Century Science*. She lives in El Cerrito, California, with her husband, a large library, and four cats.